Alfred Theophilus Lee

The Irish Church. Its Present Condition: Its Future Prospects

Alfred Theophilus Lee

The Irish Church. Its Present Condition: Its Future Prospects

ISBN/EAN: 9783337125912

Printed in Europe, USA, Canada, Australia, Japan

Cover: Foto ©Lupo / pixelio.de

More available books at **www.hansebooks.com**

THE
IRISH CHURCH.

ITS PRESENT CONDITION: ITS FUTURE PROSPECTS.

BY

THE REV. ALFRED T. LEE, M.A., LL.D.,

OF CHRIST'S COLLEGE, CAMBRIDGE, RECTOR OF AHOGHILL, AND
RURAL DEAN, DIOCESE OF CONNOR.

"Nothing short of a convulsion, tearing up BOTH Establishments by the roots, could accomplish its overthrow."—*Mr Justice Shee.*

LONDON:
WILLIAM SKEFFINGTON, 163 PICCADILLY.
DUBLIN: HODGES AND SMITH

1866.

NOTICE.

These Essays originally appeared in the pages of *The Literary Churchman*, and are now reprinted, with the hope that their publication in a collected form will be useful to those requiring information on the Irish Church question.

June, 1866.

CONTENTS.

THE
CHURCH IN IRELAND.

I.—SURVEY OF THE SUBJECT.

THE Irish Church question is daily acquiring more and more importance. The constant appearance of pamphlets and articles in reviews and newspapers on this subject shows that the public mind is awakening to a sense of the anxiety that exists for accurate information respecting it; whilst the persistence of the enemies of the Irish Church in their attack Session after Session, the formation of the Roman Catholic National Association in Dublin, and the publications respecting the Irish Church, with which the Liberation Society continues to flood the country, inaccurate and exaggerated as they are, all show that its enemies are determined to leave no stone unturned, no argument, valid or invalid, untried, in order to attain the object at which they distinctly and openly aim—the entire abolition of the Church as an Establishment in Ireland.

Now did Churchmen in England really understand the true position of the Church in Ireland were they fully alive to its past trials, its present difficulties, and the future duties that await it, could they be induced to view the subject—not as it appears on the surface, not as it is presented to them in the misleading articles of leading journals, and popular reviews—not as it appears to the jaundiced eye of political prejudice, but calmly, dispassionately, thoughtfully, and without that weariness which usually besets the

English mind, when Irish subjects are brought before it, —could this be brought to pass we have no doubt whatever that the Irish Church question would enter at once into a new phase, the clouds of misrepresentation and mis-statement which now surround it would be cleared away, and the proverbial straightforwardness and honesty of the English mind would render all the efforts of the enemies of the Irish Church—many energetic, and prodigal of their money as they are—useless and vain.

With a view, then, of bringing the present position of the Irish Church fully before our readers, we purpose in a series of essays to consider this question, being thoroughly convinced that in so doing we shall be rendering a service to the Church at large, as well as to our own Branch of it in particular.

We shall in this essay consider the question as a whole, reserving for subsequent treatment the several parts into which it may be divided.

Heavy charges are freely brought by her opponents against the Church in Ireland. It is said to be an alien Church of a small minority, thrust upon a reluctant people by the power of England in the middle of the sixteenth century; to hold property which does not justly belong to it; to be possessed of surplus revenues which might advantageously be applied to secular purposes. Its clergy are represented as rolling in wealth, with scarcely any duties to perform. Every Irishman, Roman Catholic or Protestant, is said to be compelled to contribute to its support; in a word, it is declared to be "the greatest scandal to the English Govern-"ment, and the greatest iniquity in Europe." (1)

If these charges were true, we should not have a word to

(1) Vide Circular freely distributed by the Liberation Society during the last General Election.

say in its defence; but we unhesitatingly pronounce them to be, one and all, entirely devoid of truth, as we trust to be able to prove to the satisfaction of our readers.

First. Let it ever be remembered, in considering this question, that the Established Church is *not* the English Church in Ireland. It is the old, ancient, Catholic Church of that country. The *present* Roman Catholic Church in Ireland has no real pretensions to that glorious title. It, and *not* the Irish Church, was first introduced into Ireland in the sixteenth century. The present Bishops of the Church in Ireland can trace their spiritual lineage in direct and unbroken succession to S. Patrick, the founder of the Irish Church, and from him through the Bishops of the Gallican Church to the Apostles of our Lord and Saviour (2). Not so the present Romish Bishops in Ireland. They can only, at best with doubtful steps, trace their succession in Ireland to the middle of the sixteenth century. In 1621 A.D. all the Irish sees were filled with Bishops of our communion. The whole Roman Episcopate in Ireland then consisted of only two Bishops *in partibus*, and it is well known that, at the time of the Reformation, all the Bishops then in possession of the Irish sees (with the exception of two, who, however, did not consecrate any successors), became adherents of the Reformed Faith. The present Romish Church in Ireland then cannot connect itself with the old Bishops of Ireland. The hands of the successors of S. Patrick were never laid upon them. They derive their orders from Spain and Italy, and not from the ancient Irish Church. When they first came to Ireland, they came as a foreign succession, thrust in by a foreign power, to intrude into Irish Dioceses already occupied by Irish Bishops. These

---

(2) See Wordsworth's 'Irish Church,' p. 73, and Archdeacon Hardwick's 'Church of the Middle Ages,' pp. 10—14.

foreign Bishops it was who introduced a new Episcopate into Ireland in opposition to its ancient and undoubted Episcopate, in direct contravention of the Canons of the Catholic Church. (Conc. Nicæn, Can. 8. Conc. Constant. Can. 2 and 6.)

Instead, then, of the Irish Church being, as is popularly supposed, a creature of English extraction, thrust into Ireland upon an unwilling people by English power in the 16th century, it is, in truth, of true native growth, and the old Catholic Church of Ireland, and the only religious body in that country which has any legitimate claim to that title.

When, then, an attack is made on the Established Church in Ireland, it is no modern institution, but the old Catholic Church of Ireland which is assailed, the Church of S. Patrick and S. Columkille, the Church of those Missionaries who, before S. Augustine landed in Kent, had Christianized the Highlands and the Western Isles of Scotland, and who afterwards penetrated far into England, of that Church which converted much of Europe to Christianity, and which, in modern times, has given to us an Ussher, a Bedell, a Bramhall, a Jeremy Taylor, a Magee, a Jebb, and a Mant.

The spiritual welfare of such a Church can never cease to be a subject of deepest interest to every earnest Churchman ; we are certain that its difficulties, its dangers, its necessities, need only to be pointed out to secure from the Churchmen of England willing assistance and ready aid.

And, in truth, a strange alliance of discordant elements it is that now attacks the Church in Ireland. Romish Bishops and Dissenting Ministers, the Dublin Roman Catholic National Association, and the purely Protestant Liberation Society have joined hand in hand in this campaign. Their object is, if possible, to make the Irish Church a

Government question, in order to secure the doubtful Liberals who might otherwise prefer their Church to their party. And the work goes bravely on, and will continue to do so unless Churchmen brace themselves effectually to oppose it; Churchmen we mean in England as well as Churchmen in Ireland, for the attack is really made on the former as well as on the latter. For none who of late years have watched the tactics of the Liberation Society can doubt that even in this move against the Irish Church the Church in England is the real object of attack. At present we know that their utmost exertions will be used to show that it is not so. No effort will be spared to induce Churchmen to believe that the Church in England and the Church in Ireland stand on different grounds, and that the disestablishment of the latter will rather tend to the strengthening of the former; and we are grieved to see that already some Liberal Churchmen from whom we had hoped better things have been induced to take this ground.(3) Yet surely the slightest consideration will tend to show how utterly and transparently false such reasoning is. If the Church in Ireland is once overturned, *principles* will have been established which in due time will be applied with tenfold force to the Church in England. The title by which all Church property is held, whether in England or Ireland, will have been shaken to its very foundations, mere numbers, independent of truth, intelligence, property, or education, will have been adopted as the *standard* by which an Established Church is to be judged. The right of the State to seize on the property of the Church, and appropriate it to secular purposes by its own mere motion, in opposition to the earnest protests of the Clergy and Laity of the Church, will have been successfully maintained. A solemn

(3) Vide speech of Mr J. D. Coleridge, Q.C., M.P., at his election at Exeter.

National compact, without which the Union of the two Kingdoms could never have been effected, will have been deliberately broken. English Churchmen will have been induced to desert their Irish sister at the very time of her utmost need, when with a zeal, an energy, a self-denial, such as for many years she has been a stranger to, she is bracing herself to the work to which God hath called her. And if these pernicious principles are once established with the consent of English Churchmen, *for without their consent they never can be established,* what is to prevent them being hereafter carried out to their legitimate extent and applied in all their force and cogency to the Established Church in England? Can Churchmen for a moment imagine that either Romanist or Voluntary will be satisfied with the dis-establishment of the Church in Ireland, and that they will be content to stop here? No; far from it. No sooner will the National Church in Ireland have disappeared, and the abolition of the parochial system there have handed over three-fourths of that country entirely into the hands of Rome, than with united forces, flushed with their recent triumph, they will advance with tenfold vigour against the Church in England. And when once the principles which we have mentioned above have been conceded, what is to prevent their ultimate success? If the State may rightly seize on the property of the Church and adapt it to secular purposes, why may it not do so in England as well as in Ireland? If mere numbers are to determine when a Church is and is not to be established, how for a moment, even now, can the National Church be maintained in Wales? how in any part of the country in which the Dissenting population exceeds that of the Church, *e.g.,* in Cornwall? In reply to all possible arguments that may be adduced, the Voluntary Party will say, and justly say, without possibility of rejoinder, "You "acted upon this principle in Ireland, you destroyed the "Established Church there, merely because it had not a "majority of adherents; we only ask you to do the same "in England and Wales, to carry out here the principles "which you declared to be right and just there." And under such circumstances who can doubt what the final result must be?

Nor should it be forgotten in considering this question that the Church landlords of Ireland now greatly add to the political strength of the Church in the House of Commons; but if the Irish branch of the United Church is disestablished, can we expect that the Irish landlords, who would still have to pay the existing rent-charge to some secular purpose, and upon whom then would principally fall the maintenance of the remaining Clergy of the Church, would be very warm in their support of the English branch of the then disunited Church? At present the Church has enough to do to return a majority of members in England favourable to her existence as an Establishment. The Scotch members are almost universally opposed politically to all Establishments, and should the Irish members be of the same mind, how long would the Church as an Establishment exist in England?

We have stated the matter thus plainly, because this question has been surrounded by such clouds of misrepresentation and false statement that we wish Churchmen to see clearly the issue that lies before them, and then to judge for themselves as to what their duty is with respect to it.

Again, in considering this question let us be careful to remember the true object of this attack, lest we lead away from the real question at issue. It is the abolition of the Irish Church as an Establishment, and not its reform, that is distinctly and openly sought. Spoliation under the name of reform has already been carried to such an extent in the Irish Church, that if it is carried much further it must soon cease to exist as an Establishment altogether. Ten Bishoprics suspended, 25 per cent. of the revenues of the Clergy confiscated, a heavy tax in addition imposed on their annual income, Church rates abolished, (4) a subsequent forfeiture of 12,500*l.* a year by the non-payment of Ministers' money ; these are some of the wise and gentle reforms to which the Irish Clergy have of late years been subject, till, in the words of the Archbishop of Armagh, "their incomes have been pared down to the lowest sum "compatible with the existence of the Church in this "country."—(Charge of 1864, p. 11.)

It is abolition, then, and not reform that her enemies openly seek for. "We *demand* the disendowment of the "Established Church in Ireland," say the Roman Catholic Bishops at their meeting in Dublin on December 29, 1864, although in 1826, *before* the passing of the Roman Catholic Emancipation Act, they had solemnly sworn "that they "would not exercise any privilege to which they are, or "may be entitled to disturb and weaken the Protestant "religion and Protestant Government in Ireland ;" and the Liberation Society re-echoes the cry, "It hails with "great satisfaction the renewal of the agitation for the "*abolition* of the Irish Church Establishment (5) ;" and Sir George C. Lewis ('Irish Church Question,' p. 351, ed. 1836) had long since observed that "It is ever to be "remembered in discussing the ecclesiastical state of "Ireland that the objections of the Roman Catholics to "the Established Church of that country are not of *more* "or *less;* that they would not be removed by the abolition "of a few bishoprics, or the paring down of a few benefices, "but that they lie *against its very existence.* . . . . . No "improvements in the internal economy of the Established

(4) Estimated by Lord Althorp, in 1833, to yield 90,000*l.* per annum.

(5) 'Liberator,' for Feb., 1865.

"Church, in the distribution of its revenues, or the disci-"pline of its Clergy, tend to lessen the sense of grievance "arising from this source; the objection is of *principle*, "not of *degree*, and nothing short of perfect equality in "the treatment of all religious sects will satisfy the per-"sons whose discontentment springs from this source." Subsequent experience has shown us how true these observations are, and we may be certain, however specious the statements of some of their more cautious leaders may be, that it is nothing short of the total abolition of the Irish Church as an Establishment that is now sought for by them (6).

The great impediment in the way of such a consummation is the parochial system, and, therefore, it is attacked on all sides. If once its enemies can succeed in making the system of the Church congregational instead of parochial, large tracts of country in Ireland will be left totally destitute of the ministrations of the Church (7). Many of the members of the Church in the south and west of Ireland are and must be entirely dependent for spiritual ministrations on the parochial system. By means of it they are kept together, a compact though it may be a small body, in the face of the overwhelming power of Rome. Remove the parochial system, take away the Clergy of the Church, the parish Church itself will soon be in ruins, the landlord who, in nine cases out of ten, is a Churchman also, will soon follow, and the few Protestants left without the protection of either Clergyman or Landlord must in a very few years be absorbed into the Church of Rome. This is the result which will inevitably follow the abolition of the

(6) Witness the letter of "An Irish Catholic" in the *Times* of Nov. 20, 1865:—"No tinkering, no patching, no efforts to make *the detestable nuisance* less unpalatable by softening down its particular or minor scandals can ever be accepted as a final settlement."

(7) "In the circumstances of Ireland . . . the *congregational* is the right, proper, and fitting system."—(Speech of Mr Bernal Osborne, June 26, 1863.)

parochial system in very many parts of Ireland, and when the influence of the Clergy of the Church which now pervades every part of the country shall have been removed, and the Roman Catholic priests shall thus have obtained undivided sway over the greater part of Ireland, it is easy for any one acquainted with its past history to forecast the results which ere long will surely follow, for there was never a more thorough delusion than the idea that the abolition of the Irish Church Establishment will satisfy the Roman Catholics, or pacify Ireland (8). Our own experience leads us to believe that Ireland will never really become England's difficulty till the beneficial influence of the Established Church is removed from it.

For all these reasons then, because the Irish Church is the old Catholic Church of Ireland, because its revenues are barely sufficient for the work it has to do, because it is now faithfully and diligently doing that work, because the present attack upon it is unjust, uncalled for, and plainly made subservient to purposes of party, we call upon Churchmen in general to rally round it, not to be satisfied with the "popular statements" that are current respecting it, but to EXAMINE THE FACTS OF THE CASE, FOR THEMSELVES, and not to cease their efforts till sound and correct information respecting the Church in Ireland is diffused throughout the several parishes of England. The result we confidently predict will be the creation of such a sound public opinion on the subject as will render the utmost efforts of its opponents utterly futile and vain.

---

(8) The Fenian movement proves the truth of this remark. If the Established Church was really felt to be such a grievance by the Roman Catholics of Ireland generally, as its enemies represented it to be, the Fenians would have placed it in the forefront of those institutions which they wished to have swept away. But the *Irish People* (the Fenian organ) frankly admits that Irishmen "care very little" about the Established Church, and commenting on this even the *Times*, hostile as it generally is to the Irish Church, is led to remark that "neither *the abolition of the Irish Church*, nor the establishment of tenant-right, would have prevented Fenianism."—*Times*, Sept. 27, 1865.

II.
THE PAST HISTORY OF THE IRISH CHURCH THE KEY TO ITS PRESENT POSITION.

The present position of the Church in Ireland can be fully understood by none but those who have made themselves intimately acquainted with its past history. Those who view Irish Church affairs only as they appear on the surface at the present day, without searching in the true causes of them which lie deeply hid in the history of ages past, are ready enough with their remedies for existing evils, which, if adopted, will be found only to aggravate them and make them more incurable than ever. Every month brings before the public some new and ardent Irish Church Reformer ready with his specific remedy to cure at once and for ever all the evils under which Ireland labours. The pages of the *Fortnightly Review* have of late been especially rich in suggestions of this kind. Mr Anthony Trollope assures us that, "as regards the Romish "Church in Ireland, all ill blood would be extinguished "by the simple annihilation of Church revenues." Lord Amberley naïvely tells us at Leeds, "that Bishops in Ire-"land are superfluous luxuries," whilst Mr James Godkin, the *Times*' correspondent in Dublin, in another article in the *Fortnightly*, is thoroughly convinced that Ireland may be regenerated by means of proprietary chapels, with pews let at moderate rents!

We have thus in the outset called attention to the popular views so flippantly put forth with respect to the Irish Church, that we may the more earnestly urge upon all those who are now turning their thoughts to this important question, the necessity of considering it calmly and thoughtfully, apart from party spirit and popular prejudice, bearing in mind the many difficulties which, since the Reformation, the Church in Ireland has been called upon to encounter, and the vast injury that will accrue should Parliament be induced, by any hasty or crude legislation, further to mutilate the already maimed executive of the Irish Church.

We have before shown that the present Established Church in Ireland is the only representative in that country of the Church of S. Patrick. The one great charge that is ever brought against it is, that it is not the Church of the great majority of the people. Undoubtedly this is the fact; but upon whom rests the blame? (1) Upon those who insisted on introducing the Reformation into Ireland in an English dress and in the English tongue. It was not the doctrines of the Reformation that were so hateful to the Irish people as the means that were used to disseminate them.

"It is highly probable," says Dr Todd in his valuable 'Life of S. Patrick,' p. 242, "that had the Reformation been presented to the Irish people in a Gaelic dress, and in the Gaelic language, it would have been accepted without difficulty. But, unfortunately, the reverse was the case. The Reformation was almost studiously brought into Ireland in ostentatious connection with the Church of the Pale and the English colonists: it was planted on the basis of Puritanism and iconoclastic outrage; and to this day the influence of that unhappy mistake continues to destroy the usefulness and paralyse the energies of the Irish Clergy. The reformed doctrines were regarded by the oppressed and degraded natives of Ireland as essentially English; *and accordingly they were rejected without examination*, and spurned with the detestation and abhorrence with which the English and everything coming from England

(1) See Wordsworth's 'Sermons on the Irish Church,' p. 218.

were, as a matter of course, received; and, as if effectually to prevent the Reformed faith spreading amongst the lower orders of the people, no part of the Bible was printed in the vernacular during the whole of the sixteenth century, and no edition of the Prayer Book appeared in Irish till 1608, more than seventy years after the commencement of the Irish Reformation!"

This seems not to have arisen from mere neglect, but from the deliberate policy of the Government of the day, for the Act of Uniformity (2 Eliz., cap. 2) contained the following most injudicious and mischievous clause: "That in every Church and place where the common "Minister or Priest hath not the use or knowledge of the "*English* tongue, it shall be lawful for the same common "Minister or Priest to say and use the Mattins, Evensong, "celebration of the Lord's Supper, and administration of "each of the Sacraments, and all their common and open "Prayer, in the *Latin* tongue, in the order and form men-"tioned and set forth in the Book established by this Act." In those parts of the country in which the English language was not understood the obvious substitute would have been the same Liturgy in the Irish tongue—in a language "understanded of the people." But this might not be, says the Statute, "as well for the diffi-"culty to get it printed, as that few in the realm "could read Irish letters;" and although a few years afterwards a private Clergyman was enabled to do this with marked success, the Government excused itself under the plea of inability to find persons actually qualified to read the Irish character. Had there been any real desire to teach the people in their own native tongue there would have been little difficulty in obtaining a supply of the proper types for printing, or in training suitable persons to minister to the Irish people in their own vernacular; but the disastrous policy of the day was to force the English power and the English language upon the reluctant Irish people, and for this purpose it was ordered that vacant benefices should be bestowed upon "persons who could "speak English, apt and convenient to occupy the same," and thus, whilst pastor after pastor was set over the people who could not speak a word which they could understand, can we wonder that they flocked to the ministrations of the emissaries of Rome, who spoke to them in the language which they loved? There can be but little doubt that had the people of Ireland enjoyed the use of public prayer, and the hearing of the Word of God in a language they understood; had the principles of the Reformation been carried out in that country as in England; had every parish church been provided with a Bible and a Prayer Book in the language of the people; never would the Church of Rome have regained her hold on their affections, never would Ireland have been torn by the religious animosities which have since rent her asunder.

II. But this, though the chief, was but one of the many hindrances to the spread of the doctrines of the Reformed Faith in Ireland. At the Reformation Henry VIII dissolved the monasteries in Ireland, as well as in England. At their dissolution they possessed a large portion of the tithes of the country. These were bestowed by the Crown on laymen, and have ever since been enjoyed by them Thus a great proportion of the Church property was alienated to secular uses, and to such a fearful extent was this plundering carried that 562 rectories became impropriate and 118 parishes wholly impropriate, making in all 680 parishes, whose revenues were thus alienated from ecclesiastical uses, whilst, in addition to this, 1,480 glebes passed out of the possession of the Church into the hands of laymen (2). No wonder, then, that Dr Ryves said, in his 'Poor Vicar's Plea' "that the Church of Ireland lies "buried under a heap of impropriations," and that the Convocation of 1634 declared in their address to the King (Strafford's State Papers, i. p. 382), "that in all the "Christian world the rural clergy have not been reduced "to such extremity of contempt and beggary as in this, "your Highness's kingdom, by the means of so frequent "appropriations, commendams, and violent intrusions into "their undoubted rights in times of confusion, having "the churches ruined, their habitations left desolate, "*their glebes concealed*, and by inevitable consequence, "an invincible necessity of a general non-residency "imposed upon them, whereby the ordinary subject "hath been left wholly destitute of all possible means to "learn true piety to God, loyalty to their Prince, and "civility one towards another." When Bishop Bedell took possession of his Diocese of Kilmore in 1630, he found his Cathedral Church utterly destroyed, the Bishop's residence levelled to the ground, the parish churches "all ruined, unroofed, and unrepaired," and in the two Dioceses of Kilmore and Ardagh only sixteen resident clergy. The result of his investigation he sadly communicated to Laud, "and shortly," said he, to speak much ill matter in a few words, "the state of the "Church in Ireland is very miserable." The chief cause of this deplorable condition of the Church was the enormous number of impropriate benefices that had become the property of laymen (3) ; in addition to which Bishop Jeremy

---

(2) Vide Dean Newland's 'Apology for the Irish Church,' p. 233.

(3) Carte, in his 'Life of Ormonde' (i. 63), tells us that at this time, "in the whole Province of Connaught (which, be it observed, is now the most Roman Catholic Province in Ireland) there was scarce a Vicar's pension which exceeded

Taylor tells us, in his funeral Sermon, on the death of Archbishop Bramhall: "At the Reformation the Popish "Bishops and Priests seemed to conform, and did so, that "keeping their Bishoprics they might enrich their kindred "and dilapidate the revenues of the Church, which by "pretended offices, false information, fee farms at con-"temptible rents, and ungodly abominations was made "low as poverty itself, and unfit to minister to the needs "of those that served the altar, or the noblest purposes of "religion." (Bramhall's Works. Anglo-Cath. Lib., Vol. I. lix.), and thus, whilst they outwardly conformed, they really deformed the Church of which they were the unworthy rulers.

Nor in the days of Dean Swift, seventy years after the death of Bramhall, had the state of affairs altered for the better. "The Clergy," says he, "having been stripped of "the greatest part of their revenues, the glebes being "generally lost, the tithes in the hands of laymen, the "Churches demolished, and the country depopulated, it "was necessary to unite small vicarages." (4.) And yet at this very time when Dean Swift gives this deplorable account of the poverty of the Church, the Irish Parliament did not hesitate in 1735 still further to despoil it by handing over to the laity the tithe of agistment, or pasturage, (5.) by which measure "such a diminution "of the income of the Clergy in most parts of Ireland "was produced, these several parishes had to be joined

---

forty shillings a year, and in many places they were but eighteen shillings;" and he adds (i. 299) that several of the Bishoprics "were reduced to 50*l.* a year, as Waterford, Kilfenora, and others; and some to five marks, as Cloyne and Kilmacduagh."

(4.) Swift's Works, Vol. IV., pp. 71, 72, quoted by Newland, p. 89.

(5.) Dean Swift gave vent to his indignation on the passing of this measure, in one of the last but most pungent of his satires, called the Legion Club.

"together to make out a sufficient subsistence for a "minister." (Charge of the late Primate, 1846, p. 21.)

The rapacity of the Irish landlords thus produced "those "godless combinations, commonly called Unions," which have placed under the nominal superintendence of a single pastor large tracts of country, over which it is utterly impossible that he can exercise any real supervision, and a vital and permanent injury was thus inflicted on the Church in Ireland, from which it continues to suffer to the present day. Seven, eight, and even ten parishes had of necessity to be united to form even a miserable pittance for a single minister. The Churches in the several parishes thus united, could not all be served by a single clergyman, and these, one by one, gradually fell into decay. The people in many cases having no Church left them to worship in, no Clergyman to minister to their spiritual needs, no glebe house for his residence among them, were gradually absorbed into the Church of Rome, which surrounded them on every side.

Need we be surprised that under such circumstances as these the Church in Ireland made little or no progress? Need we wonder that, having at all times a powerful and watchful enemy to oppose her from without, she now languished and grew feeble under the continued extortions of her professed members from within?

III. But in addition to those which we have already mentioned there was another grievous hindrance to the progress of the Church in Ireland. In the sixteenth century, when England found herself vexed with Puritanical teachers, she endeavoured to rid herself of them by importing them into Ireland. Travers, the opponent of Hooker, was thus advanced to the highly-important and influential post of Provost of Trinity College, Dublin. A Puritanical school was thus founded in Ireland, which has ever since exercised a powerful influence in that country. (6.) Nor must it be forgotten that soon afterwards the plantation of the Presbyterians in Ulster "disturbed the "Church's peace, impeded her progress, and diminished "her power of promoting religious improvement"—(Bp. Mant's Irish Church History, Vol. I., p. 365)—for in the north of Ireland at that time "the clearance of the Episco-"palian Clergy had been most effectual, and their places "had been supplied by the sturdiest champions of the "Covenant, taken principally from the west of Scotland, "the disciples of Cameron, Renwick, and Peden, and pro-"fessing in the wildest and most gloomy sense the austere "principles of their party." (7.) Thus another element of religious division was introduced into Ireland, and henceforth Rome fomented the division of Protestants to secure her own supremacy. (8.)

Much more might be added on this subject, but we trust enough has been said to show the manifold difficulties with which the Church in Ireland has had to contend, since the Reformation, which have impeded and effectually hindered all her efforts at extension. When, in addition to this, we remember that nearly up to the time of the passing of the Roman Catholic Emancipation Act, her chief dignities were bestowed mainly from considerations of State (a practice which has not altogether ceased), and with but little regard to the good of the Church, and that thus her strength was paralyzed, and her vigour crippled in its most vital part, we need not be surprised that the Irish Church has not advanced with

(6) See Bramhall's Works, Vol. I., p. cxiv., notes, in which the Editor shows that at that time "The Irish Church was deluged with Puritanism."

(7) Jeremy Taylor's Works, Vol. I., p. 104. Heber's Edition.

(8) On this point see especially Archdeacon Wordsworth's 'Sermons on the Irish Church,' p. 262.

rapid steps; our only wonder is that she has so effectually maintained her position in the country at all.

Such was the condition of the Irish Church at the time of the Union in 1801. By the 5th Article of the Act which united the two kingdoms, the temporalities of the two Churches of England and Ireland were placed on the same footing, the Ecclesiastical Union which had existed for centuries was further cemented by the consent of the Episcopate of both countries to this measure, and it was made the foundation of this Act, without which it never would have passed the Irish Parliament, "that the con-"tinuance and preservation of the said united Church, *as "the Established Church of England and Ireland,* should be "deemed and taken to be an ESSENTIAL AND FUNDAMENTAL "PART OF THE UNION."—The view which the Irish Bishops of that day took of this measure, how thoroughly they considered that it would identify the Church in Ireland with the Church in England, and thus effectually preserve it from attack, is evident from the letter addressed by Bishop O'Beirne, of Meath, to Lord Castlereagh, in November, 1799, enclosing a "memorandum as to the uniting and "*identifying* the Churches of England and Ireland" (9). In it the Bishop says "the local circumstances of the "Church of Ireland, *the existence and safety of which is "essential to the connexion between the two countries,* would, "in themselves require that it should incorporate and iden-"tify with the Church of England as the greatest security "it can look to, and as its most effectual preservation "against the dangers to which these circumstances may "enforce it." It is evident, then, that the Irish Episcopate agreed to the Union in the belief that the Church in Ireland

(9) See Memoirs and Correspondence of Viscount Castlereagh. Vol. iii, pp. 1, 2.

would thereby be placed in an unassailable position. How grievously they were mistaken subsequent events have shown. No sooner was the Roman Catholic Emancipation Act passed in 1829, than an active Parliamentary opposition to the Irish Church was organized. In 1834, under the pretence of reform, ten of her Bishoprics were suspended; soon after, in 1838, a fourth of her revenue was confiscated; subsequently, in 1854, she was deprived of 12,500*l.* of her annual income, by the abolition of Ministers' money, by 17 and 18 Vict., c. 11. Thus a continued process of spoliation has been carried on, till, in the words of the Primate, in his Charge of 1864, "the incomes of the Irish "clergy have been pared down to the lowest sum com-"patible with the existence of the Church in this country."

Such, then, are some of the chief causes why the Church n Ireland has not long since become the Church of the great majority of the Irish people. No sooner had she reformed herself, with the general consent of the nation, than the English Government compelled her to conduct her services in a tongue which the people could not understand, and to accept as their pastors, clergy who were totally ignorant of their language. The Bible and Prayer Book were not translated into the vernacular. Court favourites became possessed of a great part of her revenues, &c., large proportions of her tithes and glebes at once passed into their hands. Then a flood of Puritanism, imported from England and Scotland, swept over the land, quickly followed by the fearful massacres of 1641-43, in which 143,000 Protestants perishe No sooner had she in some small measure recovered from this blow, which was intended to annihilate her altogether, than the very men who should have succoured and defended her—the nobles and landlords of Ireland—in the Parliament of 1735 deprived her of the tithe of agistment, which rendered necessary that deplorable system of unions which has so long left whole districts destitute of any real spiritual superintendence from the ministrations of the Church ; add to this, that for a very long period the Church was used by the State as an instrument of Government in Ireland, that her chief dignities were bestowed from matters of policy, not with a view to the spiritual interests of the Church ; that a long series of penal laws were enacted not to protect the Church herself so much as to carry out a long-cherished but mistaken policy which subsequent experience has shown to be both impolitic and unwise, but from the effects of which, nevertheless, the Church largely suffers to this day ; when, in addition to this, we remember that no longer than thirty years since, nearly one half of her Bishoprics were suspended and a fourth of her revenue confiscated, that year after year her Bishops and Clergy are still diverted from their own proper work to that of Church defence from the Parliamentary attacks which are continually hanging over her ; when we say all these things are duly weighed, and calmly considered, the wonder is, not that the Church in Ireland has not advanced more rapidly in numbers, but that amidst so many difficulties and discouragements, with ever-watchful foes without, and too often lukewarm and indifferent friends within, she has been enabled to maintain so faithfully, and so well, the difficult, and often embarrassing position which in the Providence of God she is called to fill.

III.

SYNODS OF THE CHURCH IN IRELAND.

It was a wise remark of the late lamented Baptist von Hirscher, in his treatise on "the State of the Church," published some sixteen years ago, that "the revival of "Synodical institutions so long demanded is nothing else "than a product of the universal spirit of the age" (p. 125). The subsequent revival of full synodical action in the Provinces of Canterbury and York, the earnest though as yet unavailing efforts made by the whole Irish Episcopate to remove the enforced silence of their Convocation, the growing desire in all religious bodies for mutual consultation amongst their religious teachers, shows how strongly the spirit to which Von Hirscher alluded has of late years made itself felt. But the peculiar circumstances in which the Irish Church is now placed, the unceasing and unjust attacks which are made upon her, make it a crying injustice that the Government of the day should deliberately refuse permission to her Bishops and Clergy to assemble together in Synod, and consider such measures as may be requisite for the common good. Complaints are most unjustly made against the Irish Clergy, for not proposing schemes of internal reform, and yet the only available means by which they can rightly and orderly do so is denied them. And this injustice is the more keenly felt by the Irish Clergy, because the liberty which is refused to them is freely granted to the other religious bodies which surround them. They are refused permission to deliberate in Synod on matters in which they feel the deepest personal interest, and which greatly concern the present and future welfare of the Church in Ireland. And yet Synod after Synod is convened without let or hindrance by the Irish Legate of the Pope, and no word of disapprobation is heard, and every year the General Assembly of the Presbyterians is held for the regulation of their spiritual and temporal affairs, and no voice of remonstrance is raised against it. How much longer, then, are the Clergy of the Church to be denied those rights which are freely granted to Romish Priests and Presbyterian Ministers?

But we are fully persuaded that the day is not far distant when this strange anomaly will be removed. Churchmen in Ireland are becoming more and more resolved not to cease their labours till they have secured the restoration of their Synodical action, and Churchmen in England will, we are sure, gladly give them a helping hand. Either the long-suffering patience of the Irish Primates will at length be exhausted, and they will succeed in overcoming the scruples of their Suffragans, which is now understood to be the chief obstacle to their summoning their Provincial Synods, *ex mero motû*, without any Royal writ—which they have an undoubted right to do—or the united voice of Churchmen will so imperatively demand that the Irish Church shall no longer be treated with manifest injustice, that the Government will be obliged to yield to pressure from without, and tardily grant that, which now they might gracefully accede to.

Yet whatever the means may be by which Synodical action shall at length be restored to the Church in Ireland, it cannot but be interesting to us at this crisis briefly to consider the past history of her Synods, and the true state of the question at the present moment.

In considering it we must always carefully bear in mind, that, although Christianity was introduced into Ireland by

S. Patrick about the middle of the fifth century, it was not till *six* centuries afterwards that Ireland was divided into Dioceses, or that Bishops in it exercised Diocesan jurisdiction (1).

The Irish Church was originally planted in a heathen land, and for some centuries was surrounded by a very gross form of heathenism. The consecration of Bishops without sees was therefore at first a matter of necessity, nor was this irregular whilst their duties were essentially missionary. Indeed, the missionary Bishops of Melanesia and Central Africa in our own day, occupy a somewhat similar position. But it would be a great error to suppose that because there was no Diocesan Episcopacy in the early Irish Church, that the distinction between the orders of Priest and Bishop was not thoroughly understood and carefully preserved. Dr Todd, in the introduction to his 'Life of S. Patrick,' has abundantly proved that in Ireland at this period Bishops alone consecrated Churches, ordained Priests and Deacons, administered the rite of Confirmation, and consecrated other Bishops. (2.) But of necessity the early Irish Bishops resided chiefly in monasteries, for in such a state of society as that in which they lived, a Christian life was scarcely possible, except in a community exclusively Christian. In process of time such communities were formed in various localities throughout Ireland, and became the centres of civilization and religion to the surrounding districts. But these establishments were often isolated and at a distance from each other, and each therefore had to provide the means of obtaining all the rites of the Church, whether episcopal or priestly, for all those who resided within its walls. " Hence

---

(1) See especially R. King's 'Early History of the Primacy of Armagh,' pp. 1-10.

(2) Todd's 'S. Patrick,' p. 5.

"arose the monastic Bishop of the Scotic religious houses." The Abbot or Superior may have been a Presbyter only, or a layman, or, as in the case of S. Brigid and her dependent abbesses, even a woman. But a Bishop was always connected with the Society, although without Diocese or jurisdiction, and bound, like other inmates of the monastery, to render an absolute obedience to his monastic Superior. (3.) It is probable, however, that in time the jurisdiction of the monastic Bishops gradually extended itself over the minor religious houses in connection with the original monastery, and moreover, when any of the petty Kings or chieftains embraced Christianity, they provided one or more Bishops for their clans, in addition to the other Clergy. The district of country which owed allegiance to the chieftain thus became the proper sphere of labour of the Bishop and his Clergy, and this was the first approach to Diocesan or territorial jurisdiction in Ireland. The island was at this time subdivided into a great number of petty principalities, and these were grouped into two great confederacies, one of which comprehended the northern, the other the southern portion of Ireland. These two primary divisions led afterwards to the establishment of the two original Archbishoprics of Armagh and Cashel, whilst the suffragan Bishops had jurisdiction equal in extent to the dominion of their chief. (4.) The present dioceses of Dromore, Kilmacduagh, Kilfenora, Ossory, and Ross, are nearly co-extensive with the former territories of ancient Irish clans.

During the whole of this period, however, in which there

---

(3) Dr Todd's 'S. Patrick,' pp. 37, 38.

(4) See Dr Reeves' Ecclesiastical Antiquities of 'Down and Connor,' p. 126, who remarks that the same practice prevailed in England in the seventh century, when, according to Bede, there were not more than seven Bishops in all the Heptarchy.

were no fixed Dioceses, or regularly defined parishes, a vigilant system of Episcopal visitation was kept up, and one of the chief reasons for these constant visitations would seem to be, the opportunities they afforded for obtaining contributions from Churches and people. "From early "times," Dr Reeves tells us, (5), "till the tenth century, it "was the custom for the Bishop personally to visit each "parish under his jurisdiction, once a year, unless when the "Diocese was of too great an extent, in which case the "indulgence of a biennial, or at farthest, a triennial visita-"tion, was allowed him and many specific instances of "such visitation are given in his introduction to Primate "Colton's visitation of Derry in A.D., 1397."

Considerable doubts exist as to the authenticity of the Canons ascribed to a Synod, said to have been held by S. Patrick in A.D. 459, although they are given by Wilkins in the first volume of his *Concilia* (6), but there is no doubt that in the early ages of Irish Church history when occasion arose for the settlement of any matters of doctrine or Ecclesiastical discipline, they were determined by a Synod of Bishops and Clergy. Such a Synod was held by S. Columkille at Drumcheatt, in A.D. 590, which was attended by twenty Bishops and forty Priests, and in A.D. 634. The celebrated Synod of the "White Field" was held near Leighlin to determine the observance of Easter (7).

The anomalous system of unbeneficed Bishops continued to exist in Ireland to the beginning of the twelfth century. The first step towards removing it was taken at the Synod of Rathbreasil (now Mountrath, in the Queen's County) held in A.D. 1110. At this Synod for the

---

(5) 'Eccles. Antiquities of Down and Connor,' pp. 98, 99.

(6) See Todd's 'S. Patrick,' pp. 485-489.

(7) King's 'Irish Church History,' i. 86 and 171.

first time the Legate of the Pope presided in an Irish Council; Gillebert, Bishop of Limerick, acting in that capacity. It was chiefly occupied in forming a regular Diocesan system throughout Ireland, and in fixing the boundaries of the several Dioceses. It was determined at this Council that, exclusive of Dublin (8), Ireland should be divided into twenty-four Dioceses, twelve in the north, subject to the Archbishop of Armagh, twelve in the south, subject to the Archbishop of Cashel. But this arrangement was soon afterwards superseded by the Synod of Kells in A.D. 1152, when the Dioceses of Ireland were distributed into four provinces, under the four Archbishops of Armagh, Cashel, Dublin, and Tuam.

Previous to the twelfth century, then, we must not expect to hear of Provincial Synods in Ireland, since before that period there was no Metropolitan jurisdiction, properly so called, exercised in the Irish Church, but since that time these Synods became frequent (9). In a valuable letter of Archbishop King, of Dublin, to Archbishop Wake, dated September 12, 1717, he speaks of the affairs of the Church previous to the Reformation being conducted, "sometimes, though rarely, in National Synods, and *fre-* "*quently* in Provincial and Diocesan." "In these," he continues, "I conceive were transacted and ordered the "spiritual concerns of the Church, and we have still "remaining several constitutions made in them. The

---

(8) This See was left subject to the Archbishop of Canterbury. The Bishops of the Danish towns of Dublin, Limerick, and Waterford were for about a century subject to the Metropolitan jurisdiction of the English Primate and consecrated by him. Hence arose the first connexion between Ireland and the See of Rome.

(9) A List of such Synods held in the different Provinces of Ireland down to the time of the Reformation will be found in Dr A. J. Stephens', Q.C., learned opinion on the 'Provincial Synod of Armagh,' p. 18.

"Provincial Synods were triennial and the Diocesan "annual. The first is dropped in the other three "Provinces, but has all along been kept up in that of "Dublin, and is still, according to this ancient custom, "and at it appear all the Bishops of the Province, the "Deans, Archdeacons, and Proctors for the Chapters, and "other Clergy." His Grace further observes, "The Clergy "of Ireland never made such a submisson as the Clergy "of England did to Henry VIII., nor have we, that I "know of, any law making it penal to us to make Provincial "Constitutions. We have several of these Constitutions "remaining, and an account of the Synods that exacted "them" (10).

We have abundant evidence then that Provincial Synods were commonly held in Ireland previous to the sixteenth century. We shall consider subsequently the manner in which the Irish Church accepted the Reformation, and conclude our present remarks with a few observations respecting the Ecclesiastical union that existed between the Churches of England and Ireland, previous to the union of these Establishments in 1800.

At the celebrated Synod of Cashel, held in A.D. 1172, at which three Archbishops and twenty-eight Bishops were present, it was decreed "that all Divine matters shall for "the future in all parts of Ireland be regulated after the "model of Holy Church, according to the observance of "the Anglican Church." Henceforth the offices and practices of the Church of Ireland were made to agree wherever the authority of the Council extended, with those of the Church of England, and thus the Anglican faith was introduced into Ireland, many centuries before the Reformation. Afterwards we find that frequent

(10) See 'Christian Examiner,' vol. iv., p. 182.

translations of Bishops took place from Irish sees to English sees, and *vice versâ*. Laurence O'Toole, Archbishop of Dublin, was present at the Council of Windsor in A.D. 1175, when a peace was agreed upon between the King of England and the King of Connact (Connaught) in Ireland, and Augustin, an Irishman, was nominated by the King, Bishop of Waterford (11). Henry de Londres, Archbishop of Dublin from A.D. 1213 to A.D. 1228, was present at, and advised, the signing of Magna Charta (12). And it is a fact well worthy of note that at the Council of Constance, in A.D. 1414, the Ambassadors of the French King having objected that the English Church was not entitled to vote as a separate National Church on account of the fewness of its Bishops, the English Ambassadors replied, "that the Church in England and Ireland *was one National* "*Church*, and that the number of their Bishops together "exceeded the number of the French Church" (13). The case was minutely entered into and decided by the Council in favour of England, and it is not a little curious to remark that throughout that Council the Anglican Church was represented on all committees and judicial tribunals by "Patrick, Bishop of Cork."

In accordance with the view thus taken by the Council of Constance, public documents of the date of the Reformation constantly speak of the Churches of England and Ireland as "one Church." In the Injunctions of Edward VI., issued A.D. 1547, the King is spoken of as "Defender "of the Faith, and, under Christ, of *this Church of Eng-* "*land and Ireland* the supreme head." In the Articles agreed upon by Convocation of Canterbury in 1552 the

---

(11) See Hody's 'History of Convocation,' p. 234.

(12) 'Liber Munerum Hiberniæ,' vol. ii., p. 33.

(13) Vide Labbe and Cossart's 'Concilia Generalia,' as quoted by Archdeacon Stopford in his reply to Serjeant Shee, pp. 98, 99.

same expression "Church of England and Ireland" (Ecclesia Anglicana et Hibernica) occurs (14). In the Injunctions of Queen Elizabeth "the form of bidding the "prayers" runs thus, "Ye shall pray for Christ's Holy "Catholic Church . . . . and specially for *the Church* of "England and Ireland" (15), whilst the title of the first Irish Canon of 1634 is "of the agreement of the *Church* "of England and Ireland in the profession of the same "Christian religion," and the Canon itself speaks of the agreement of the Church of Ireland with the Church of England "in the confession of the same Christian faith "and the doctrine of the Sacraments."

Since A.D. 1634 the Articles of the Irish Church have been the same as those of the English. The successive revisions of the Liturgy in the reigns of Edward VI. and Elizabeth were also adopted by the Church in Ireland The Canons of the Church in Ireland are, it is true, in some minor matters different from those of the Church in England, but in all important particulars they fully agree (16), but this difference of Canons no more prevents the Provinces of the Irish Church being in full communion with the Provinces of the English, than the difference of the Canons of the Province of York, in former times, prevented its being considered one Church with the Province of Canterbury.

The Acts of Union in 1800 made England and Ireland

---

(14) Sparrow's Collections, pp. 48, 49.

(15) Sparrow's Collections, p. 79.

(16) To this, however, there is now a noteworthy exception. Last year the Convocations of Canterbury and York repealed the 29th English Canon, and altered the Canons respecting subscription, and have thus brought the English Canons into accordance with the Statute Law. The Irish Primates memorialized the Crown for the issue of a Royal writ to enable the Irish Convocation to make similar alterations in the Irish Canons. In reply, her Majesty's Government simply ignored the existence of Irish Convocation altogether.

one United Kingdom. The Church in England and Ireland was already one Church, and recognized by the highest ecclesiastical and civil authorities as such. The two Establishments had been created by separate legislatures, and the Acts of Union did but consolidate them, and for this no canonical sanction was requisite. When the Lords Spiritual of Ireland became associated with the Lords Spiritual of England as the Parliamentary representatives of the two Churches, the Establishments were made one by statute, and the two Churches became by the law civil, what they had long been by the law Spiritual, ONE Church; and the title United Church followed as a matter of course.

IV.

SYNODS OF THE CHURCH IN IRELAND.

PART II.

THE first decisive step taken in Ireland towards establishing the Reformation was the renouncing the Supremacy of the Pope, by an act of the Irish Parliament passed in A.D. 1537. (1) Before this the oath of the King's Supremacy had been taken in A.D. 1532-34 by the Irish Bishops and Clergy. It is remarkable that the Irish chiefs quietly followed the example thus set them, and pledged themselves by solemn covenant to annihilate "the usurped authority of the "Bishop of Rome." (2) The foundation stone of the Irish Reformation was thus laid with the aid of the chief authorities both in Church and State and the expressed consent of the leaders of the people. "For it is to be noted," says Cox, "that these submissions were so universally made "all over the kingdom, that there was not a Lord, or "Chieftain of any note in Ireland but submitted in this "manner, or in like form, for they made not scruple to "renounce the Pope, when once they had resolved to obey "the King." (3) And it is of great importance that this

(1) 28 Hen. VIII., c. 2. A.D. 1536—37.

(2) The Oath of Supremacy was taken by the Irish Chiefs in 1542-44. The Earl of Desmond took it in 1540, O'Donnel's indenture, confirmed by the same oath, is dated Aug. 6, 1542, "Quod renunciabit relinquet et adnihilabit pro posse suo usurpatam authoritatem, et Primaciam Romani Pontificis." McMahon's indenture is dated Aug. 14, 1542; O'Neal's January, 1543; and most of the other chiefs followed in the course of that year. O'More's is dated May 13, 1543, O'Kelly's May 24, O'Rourke's Sept. 1, 1543.—See Cox's Hib. Angl. p. 272, 273.

(3) Cox, p. 274.—See also Palmer on the Church, i., 423.

should be borne in mind at a time when the most unscrupulous statements are being made respecting the manner in which the Reformation was first established in Ireland. In 1551 A.D. Edward VI. sent an order to the Lord Deputy Sir Anthony St Leger, for the use of the English Liturgy in all the Parish Churches of Ireland. Before he issued his proclamation, the Lord Deputy called "an assembly of "the Archbishops and Bishops, together with the other "Clergy of Ireland," and it was then agreed by a majority of the Synod (the Primate, however, and his Suffragans who were present dissenting) that the English Liturgy should be accepted. It was accordingly first used at Christ Church Cathedral, on Easter Day 1551, on which occasion a Sermon was preached by Archbishop Browne of Dublin.

In the reign of Queen Elizabeth, her Majesty signified her pleasure to Lord Sussex, then Lord Deputy, for a general meeting of the Clergy and the establishment of the Protestant religion. At this time Convocation, in the modern sense of the term, did not exist in Ireland, but the ancient Synod of the Clergy had the power of settling all matters respecting religion. "It would appear," says Dr Elrington's *Life of Ussher*, p. 41, "that the dissimilarity "of the proceedings in England and Ireland with respect "to the Reformation arose from the different constitution "of the two Churches. In England the Convocation "originally instituted for the purpose of managing the "temporal concerns of the Clergy, had gradually usurped "the power of the Provincial Synod, and become the in-"strument of framing Articles and Canons for the Church. "In Ireland the Provincial Synod had not been super-"seded, and by their consent given at three different times, "in the reign of Edward, when summoned by Sir Anthony "St Leger, in the third of Elizabeth called together by Lord "Sussex, and in the year 1565 by Sir Henry Sydney, the

"Clergy received the use of the English Liturgy, and ex-"pressed their conformity to the doctrines of the English "Church. . . . The Reformation then in Ireland was "thus carried on by the regular assembly to which affairs "of the Church ought canonically to be entrusted."

It was not till the year 1615 that a Convocation, similar to that now existing in the English provinces, was assembled in Ireland. Previous to this, the Ecclesiastical affairs of the country had been transacted principally, in provincial, but occasionally, in national Synods. James I., however, when in 1603 he summoned an Irish Parliament, convoked with it also a Convocation. Archbishop Jones of Dublin was its President, and Randolph Barlow, Archdeacon of Meath, was Prolocutor of the Lower House. The records of this Convocation have perished, but we know from other sources that Articles of Religion, 104 in number, and divided into nineteen heads, were drawn up and agreed upon. They were strongly Calvinistic in their character, but they were not confirmed by Letters Patent under the Great Seal, and they were shortly afterwards superseded by the Canons passed in 1634, and which accepted the XXXIX English Articles of 1562.

Nineteen years elapsed before another Irish Parliament was summoned in 1634, and with it was also summoned the Convocation. It was convened by provincial writs, dated May 24, 1634. Archbishop Ussher was its President; Henry Leslie, Dean of Down, was Prolocutor of the Lower House. This Convocation enacted those Canons which are still in force at the present day. The first Canon is entitled "Of the agreement of *the Church* of England and Ireland "in the profession of the same Christian religion." It adopted the XXXIX Articles *verbatim et literatim*, and declared the agreement of the Irish Church with the Church of England "in the Confession of the same Christian faith "and the doctrine of the Sacraments." These Canons were 100 in number, and were drawn up by Bramhall, then Bishop of Derry ; they are for the most part the same as the English, but are arranged in a different order. Some differences, however, not altogether unimportant, exist between them. (4)

The Convocation again met in 1636 and 1640, but no other than ordinary business seems to have been transacted during these sessions. In the reign of Charles II. only one Parliament was summoned. Convocation met May 10, 1661, Bramhall, now Primate, was its President. Dr Mossom, Dean of Christchurch, was Prolocutor of the Lower House. (5) In this Convocation the revised edition of the 'Book of Common Prayer' was considered and approved of, previous to its being sanctioned by the act of Uniformity, 17 and 18 Charles II. cap. 6. The approval of this Prayer-Book by the Convocation is set forth in the preamble to this statute, which thus recognized the Constitutional status of Convocation. During the reign of William III. two Parliaments were held in Ireland, but the Convocation of the Clergy was not convened. Neither during the first ten years of this monarch's reign were the Convocations of Canterbury and York permitted to transact any business.

Queen Anne summoned a Parliament in 1703. Convocation met along with it, but as they had been summoned

---

(4) For points of difference with the English Canons, see 'Mant's Irish Church History,' I., pp. 497—504 ; and an excellent Edition of the Irish Canons, published by the Association for Discountenancing Vice, and edited by Dr Studdert.

(5) This Convocation is described in (14 and 15 Charles II., c. 24), A.D. 1662, as "consisting of the Prelates and Clergy of this Church and kingdom of Ireland, called together out of the several provinces of Armagh, Dublin, Cashel, and Tuam, by the authority of your Highness's writ, and orderly assembled in a national Synod or Convocation," and is thus recognized as an integral part of the Constitution.

only under the "præmunientes" clause in the Bishop's writs, they refused to transact business till they were summoned by the authority of their Metropolitans under the provincial writs, and thus were formed into "a truly "Ecclesiastical Synod." The Archbishops and Bishops accordingly addressed the Lord-Lieutenant in a memorial in which "they insisted on the Church's rights to have a "full Convocation with every Parliament," and begged that her Majesty would issue the provincial writs to the four Archbishops, that thus they might obtain their "civil "and undoubted rights." The provincial writs were accordingly issued, and Convocation commenced its sittings on January 11, 1704. Marsh, Archbishop of Armagh, was President, and Dr Synge, Dean of Kildare, was Prolocutor. This Convocation continued its sessions till 1711. In that year the Royal license was obtained to treat and conclude upon Canons, and accordingly five Canons were enacted on November 7, 1711, one of which relates to a form of prayer for the visitation of prisoners, and the other to forms for receiving converts from the Church of Rome. This was the last act of the Irish Convocation ; it has not since met for the despatch of business.

In 1717 the Convocation of Canterbury, in consequence of its proceedings against Bishop Hoadley, was prorogued, and for 130 years the Convocation of the English and Irish provinces were in abeyance. Of late years the Convocations of Canterbury and York have renewed their active functions, and are now regularly convened with every session of Parliament. But a like measure of justice is still denied the Convocation of the Irish provinces. They are not permitted to meet and transact business, and even the very existence of such a body is authoritatively denied. It becomes therefore necessary to consider this matter somewhat carefully.

We have seen that the Irish Convocation was fully recognized as a constitutional body from the reign of James I. to that of Queen Anne. Early in the reign of George II., Primate Boulter mentions (6) that the holding of a Convocation was under consideration, but that the Cabinet were not favourable to it. This was in 1727. In 1793 an Irish Act of Parliament, 33 Geo. III., c. 29, was passed, now commonly called the Convention Act. From the operation of this Act, "the Houses of Convoca-"tion duly summoned by the King's writ" are specially exempted. By this Act of Parliament, therefore, the Irish Convocation is distinctly recognized as a lawful and constitutional assembly actually existing, although at that time in abeyance, and it was then eighty-two years since it had met for actual business. If, then, the Irish Convocation existed in 1793, after a silence of eighty-two years, what prevents it being in existence in 1865, after a silence of 154 years? The mere lapse of time cannot cause the extinction of a constitutional body, it requires some distinct act of the Legislature to terminate its existence. And where will that Act be found? not in the Act of Union, for although by it the two Churches of England and Ireland were united into our Protestant Episcopal Church, yet it did not deprive the Convocations of Canterbury and York of their separate existence; and, therefore, neither did it terminate the existence of the Irish Convocation. In England, previous to the union, there were two separate and independent Convocations in the one Church of England. Since the Act of Union there have been three Convocations in the United Church of England and Ireland, and the co-existence of three Convocations in one Church is no more inconsistent with unity since the Union than

(6) Letters. Vol. I., p. 166.

the co-existence of two Convocations in England was before it took place.

Neither will it be found that the Church Temporalities Act (3 and 4, William IV, c. 37) in any way interferes with the existence of Irish Convocation. By that Act the Crown, as the fountain of all jurisdiction within the realm, with the consent of both Houses of Parliament, transferred the jurisdiction of the Archbishops of Tuam and Cashel, on the next vacancy of those Sees, to the Archbishops of Armagh and Dublin for the time being, "with all the *metropolitan rights*, privileges, franchises, "duties, *powers and authorities* theretofore exercised" (sec. 46), and thus a union of provinces took place, and the metropolitan rights of the Archbishops of Armagh and Dublin were extended over the former provinces of Tuam and Cashel, but this in no way deprived the Bishops and Clergy of those provinces of their right to sit in Convocation, or in any way interfered with its existence as a constitutional body. There are no other Acts of Parliament which refer at all to the Irish Convocation.

We cannot then conceive what induced her Majesty's present Government to come to the conclusion contained in the letter addressed by Sir George Grey to the Irish Primates, on July 5, 1865, in reply to the urgent request, "that it would be an act of justice and in strict "accordance with the principle of the Act of Union to "issue the like writs as were issued to convene the Irish "Convocation down to the year 1714."

"I have brought this subject," writes the Home Secretary, "under the consideration of her Majesty's "Government, and I have to inform your Grace that *if* "*there existed* a Convocation of the Branch of the Esta- "blished Church in Ireland, or a Convocation of each, or "one of the provinces of that branch of the Established

"Church summoned from time to time by writ, as is the "case with the Provincial Convocation of Canterbury and "York, her Majesty's Government are not aware of any "ground upon which a different course should be taken "with regard to such a body, from that which have been "taken with regard to the English Convocation. But as "this is not the case, her Majesty's Government do not "feel it to be their duty to advise her Majesty to call "*such a body into existence.*"

In this reply to the Primate, the Irish Convocation is assumed to have lost its existence, because the Royal writ for its assembling has not been regularly issued. Surely the omission or disuse of a mere formality through the fault of the Government, cannot abrogate an undoubted right, or dissolve a constitutional body. The Royal writs were not issued to the Irish Convocation from 1661 to 1703, and yet in the latter year the Irish Convocation was again duly assembled. The Royal writ, it is true, has not been issued from 1714 to 1866. Yet this cannot *of itself* be any real bar to the Irish Convocation being forthwith assembled. If the Royal writ was forthwith issued to the Irish Primate, the Irish Convocation could hold without any delay its regular sessions to consider questions vitally important to the Church in Ireland at the present time. But as things now stand, whilst the enemies of the Irish Church are allowed the greatest liberty "to meet and pass resolutions *demanding* the "disendowment of the Established Church," the Irish Bishops and Clergy are refused permission to exercise their undoubted constitutional rights, and consider such measures as will most conduce to her welfare and efficiency. We fear the present "Liberal" Government have other reasons than those ostensibly put forward for thus restraining the freedom of the subject, and refusing liberty "of speech "and debate" to the Irish Clergy. Irish Churchmen are at present the best abused and most maligned body in the British Empire, and it is deemed consistent with good government and fair dealing to force into silence the only body which from its knowledge and position can speak the real truth in this matter, and thus dissipate the unreasonable prejudices which are fast gathering round the Irish Church question.

Neither can it be said that the Irish Bishops and Clergy have been inert in this matter. For years past they have been unsuccessfully urging upon the Government their right to meet in Synod to consider the affairs of the Church. The first step towards the revival of Synodical action in Ireland was taken by the Down and Connor Diocesan Conference Committee in 1861, presenting to the late Primate a memorial requesting his Grace to take such steps as he and the Archbishop of Dublin might deem fit to secure "that the voice of the Irish provinces of the "United Church should be heard in Convocation." This was followed in August, 1861, by a memorial from ALL the Irish Archbishops and Bishops to her Majesty, "praying "that she would be graciously pleased to refer all matters, "involving any alteration in the doctrine, worship, disci-"pline, or government of the Church, to the consideration "of *a General Synod of the United Church of England "and Ireland*," to which memorial Sir George Grey replied that "her Majesty's Government have not felt it to "be their duty to advise her Majesty to convene a general "Synod of the Church of England and Ireland."

In November, 1862, another memorial from the Irish Prelates was forwarded to the Government by the present Primate, praying "that equal privileges with those which "have been granted to the Prelates and Clergy of the Eng-"lish provinces should be extended to the Prelates and

"Clergy of the Irish provinces," and that "therefore your "Majesty will be graciously pleased to authorize *the con-"vening of the Irish Convocation* to the end that the Pre-"lates and the representatives of the Clergy may be afforded "an opportunity of considering in Sacred Synod, such mat-"ters as may tend to the advancement of true religion, and "thereby aid in promoting joint and harmonious action on "the part of the several provinces of the United Church." To this memorial of the Archbishops and Bishops of the Irish Church, Sir George Grey simply and curtly replied "that it had been received and laid before her Majesty."

Nothing deterred by this pertinacious refusal of the Government of the constituted rights of the Irish Clergy, the Primate proceeded to have an elaborate statement of the past history and present position of the Irish Convocation drawn up, which he laid before Sir George Grey in March 1863. No result having followed from this, his Grace took the further step of obtaining in Jan. 1864 the opinion of that eminently learned civilian Dr A. J. Stephens, Q.C., who has made Irish Ecclesiastical matters his own special study and peculiar domain—as to his power "as Metropolitan without any authorization from the "Sovereign, to convene, when, and as often as he thinks "fit, a Provincial Synod of Armagh." In an elaborate opinion, which is worthy of careful study, Dr Stephens discussed the whole question, and arrived at the undoubted conclusion that in the present state of the law, his Grace does possess the power of summoning whenever he may see fit, *ex mero motu*, his own Provincial Synod. This opinion in Feb. 1864, the Primate forwarded to Sir George Grey, once more reminding him that the interests of the Irish required that the Irish Convocation should be convened, and that "it is not a new or unprecedented thing that is "sought for; it is the restoration of a privilege which the

"Church in Ireland has been in the enjoyment of under "former Sovereigns." What more reasonable, more respectful request could be made by a subject to a Sovereign? A venerable Primate placed at the head of a branch of the Church exposed to continual assault and misrepresentation, careful and watchful over the flock committed to his charge, prays that the Bishops and Clergy of that Church may be permitted to deliberate under Royal writ, on such measures as will best promote its welfare and efficiency; and permission to do this is absolutely refused by the Crown through the medium of its responsible advisers. "After "full deliberation they had been unable," writes Sir George Grey, in March, 1864, "to arrive at the conclusion that "any sufficient ground exists for taking this course, whilst "on the other hand, they apprehend that some practical "inconvenience might result from it." No "sufficient "ground" for reviving the Irish Convocation when the whole Irish Episcopate assures her Majesty that the interests of their branch of the Church demand it! Surely it was unreasonable to expect that justice should be done to the moderate demands of the Irish Bishops and Clergy, when some "practical inconvenience" might arise to the Liberal Government from the offence that might thus be given to its illiberal supporters on the other side of the Channel.

One more effort has been made by the Irish Primates to revive the action of their Convocation, but made in vain. The English twenty-ninth Canon of 1603 is the same as the sixteenth Irish Canon of 1634. When, therefore, the former was repealed by the English Convocation under Royal licence, and a new Canon enacted in its place, the Irish Primate deemed it a favourable opportunity for asking that a similar privilege might be extended to the Irish provinces of the *united* Church. But this untoward persistence of the Irish Primates in demanding that the same measure of justice should be dealt out to the Irish Clergy as to the English was too much for the patience of the Cabinet, and Sir George Grey was instructed to inform the Irish Metropolitans that they were mistaken in supposing that the Irish Clergy have any Convocation, and that, in fact, such a body does not exist.

Such is the manner in which the present Government have thought fit to treat one of the gravest of constitutional questions—the rights of the Clergy of the National Church of Ireland to deliberate on matters concerning its own welfare. By a national compact enacted in the most solemn form of statute law, the English and Irish provinces of the United Church were placed on a footing of perfect equality. The like privileges secured to one, were secured also to the other. This was especially stipulated by the Irish Parliament as the foundation of the Acts of Union. After nearly a century and a half of silent inactivity, the English provinces of the United Church are permitted under Royal writ to meet and deliberate on such subjects as they deem necessary, and under Royal licence to alter and amend various Canons relating to matters equally affecting both branches of the Church. The Irish Bishops and Clergy "humbly trusting that their long and patient "forbearance in times past will not now be regarded as "prejudicing the claim of the Irish provinces of the "United Church to obtain equal privileges with those "which have been granted to the English provinces" (7) ask permission to do the same. This permission is again and again peremptorily refused them, and at last the Irish Primates were told that they are quite mistaken in

(7) See 'Memorial of Primate to Sir George Grey,' p. 12. Parliamentary paper 258. Session 1863.

supposing that the Irish Convocation exists at all. It is hard to realize that in this 19th century, under the present British Constitution, such a body of men as the Irish Bishops and Clergy could have been treated by any government in the manner above described.

It may be thought by some that the Irish Primates have the remedy in their own hands, and that they should at once proceed to summon, *ex mero motu*, their own Provincial Synods. They might do this, but their power of *action* in these Synods, when assembled, would of necessity be very limited. Their moral influence would undoubtedly be great. They might debate such questions as concerned the present welfare of the Irish Church, and thus effectually inform the public mind on the subject; they might also do much toward considering and recommending any measures of internal reform for promoting the real efficiency of the Church. But it is more than doubtful whether, without the Royal writ, they could alter and repeal Canons enacted under it, or whether the separate Provincial Synods of Armagh and Dublin have the power, even when acting concurrently, to alter Canons enacted in a Convocation of all the provinces of the Irish Church. The real question, however, at issue is this,—the Irish Bishops claim that whatever constitutional status is given to the Convocation of the English provinces by the Royal writ, the same constitutional status should, as a matter of right and justice, be extended to the Irish Convocation also. This the Government at present persistently refuse to grant.

V.

THE TRUE POSITION OF THE ROMAN COMMUNION IN IRELAND.

THERE is nothing of which it is so difficult to disabuse the public mind as a popular error. The fallacy may be made as clear as the day. It may be shown that it rests upon a misapprehension of the true facts of the case, and is altogether without any solid foundation ; and although a thoughtful few may be thus convinced of the falseness of the popular delusion which has so long held sway, yet the many continue to believe in it, it will crop up again and again, and be repeated and believed in without examination and without inquiry. Arguments are built upon it, conclusions are drawn from it, as if it were a certain and infallible truth, and thus even grave questions of state policy will sometimes be determined on grounds wholly untenable, and which will be found upon examination to be altogether devoid of real and substantial existence.

Such a popular error is the wide-spread belief that the present Roman Communion in Ireland is the old Catholic Church of that country.

Nothing, perhaps, is more firmly believed in by most persons than this. In considering the question in popular articles and reviews, it is presumed to be an axiom which cannot be disputed, yet nothing can be more thoroughly contrary to the real facts of the case. At this time, then, when the Irish Church question is exciting so much interest, and is likely to become daily of greater importance, it will be well for us to look into this matter, and examine for ourselves what is the true position of the Church of Rome in that country.

It has ever been the misfortune of Ireland that the true source of the evils with which she is afflicted has rarely been ascertained. Successive governments, anxiously desirous to signalise their term of office by remedying what at the time seemed a crying evil, have hastily concocted remedies for supposed abuses, which in the end have created greater abuses than those which they were designed to remedy. There is no doubt that we Englishmen require great patience when discussing any Irish question above all when discussing the question of the Irish Church. It is so easy to seize on the salient points of a case and to cry out that this and that is a glaring abuse, of which such and such a plan is an evident remedy, and it is so long, and tedious, and withal with most of us, so unwelcome a task, to trace out the real causes of the evils, from which Ireland has suffered long and is suffering still ;—and the more so because these causes are really historic, and require much thought and patient inquiry to discover ;—so that there is great danger lest, in these days of rapid and eager progress, the legislature should be induced to adopt some crude and half-considered measure, which will increase rather than diminish the many undoubted evils under which Ireland at present labours, not the least of which is the total misapprehension by many of the true position which the Established Church holds in that country.

That position is as follows :—The Christian Church was first effectually founded in Ireland by S. Patrick in the fifth century. For more than 700 years after S. Patrick first preached in Ireland the Church he founded was unconnected with, and independent of, the See of Rome. In the twelfth century, Henry II. conquered Ireland, and brought

Ireland's Church for the first time under the jurisdiction of the Roman See. It was then that England introduced Popery into Ireland, and for three centuries and a half from that time, the Church of S. Patrick was subjected to the Church of Rome. But in the sixteenth century Ireland's Church rejected this foreign supremacy, and at the same time returned to the state of primitive purity of doctrine which had existed centuries before the Anglican conquest. The Pope was thus left without any Communion in Ireland to acknowledge his Supremacy, and although for some years he permitted this state of things to continue, he at length introduced a succession of foreign Bishops in Ireland from Italy and Spain, and intruded them into Sees already in the possession of the Bishops of Ireland's ancient Church. Thus did the present Roman Communion in Ireland first begin. Foreign Bishops, consecrated in foreign lands, assumed to themselves the position of the lawful Bishops of Ireland, and from *these foreigners*, and not from the Bishops of the Church of S. Patrick, does the present Roman Catholic Episcopate in Ireland derive its succession. Not one of the present Irish Roman Catholic Bishops can show any connexion with Ireland's ancient Church, whilst every Bishop of the Established Church there can trace back his Apostolic commission in clear and unbroken succession to the Apostle of Ireland himself.

It is evident, then, that whether Established or disestablished the Irish branch of the United Church is the old Catholic Church of Ireland. Men may doubt or deny this, but the fact remains. The Church which is now the Established Church of that country is the same Church that existed in Ireland before the Reformation, before the conquest of Henry II, down to the days of S. Patrick. Through all these long ages it has preserved an unbroken continuity of existence, and the body corporate that now possesses the small remaining portion of the existing revenues of the once richly endowed Church of Ireland is the same body corporate as received those lands from the hands of the ancient Lords and Chieftains of Ireland, which some of its Bishops to this day enjoy. Wars, confiscations, and rebellions have swept over and desolated that unhappy land, but Ireland's Church has remained the same through all, its energies weakened, its powers for good crippled, by ever-active foes without and too often by designing friends within, but the same Church still, the Church which gained for Ireland the far-famed title of "the Isle of Saints," the only Church which still bears witness in that land alike to Apostolic truth and Apostolic order.

Nor should we forget that it is only of late years that the Roman Communion of Ireland has publicly assumed to itself the title of *the* Catholic Church in Ireland. However pertinaciously the Roman Catholic Bishops may have claimed that title in private—though in no true sense did it ever belong to their Church — they were content previous to A.D. 1829 to assume the modest title of "Prelates of "the Roman Communion in Ireland," but no sooner had the passing of the Emancipation Act opened out to them Parliamentary influence and Parliamentary power, than they at once assumed the title of *the* Catholic Church of Ireland, and ignored altogether that Church which alone can *prove* its right to that venerable title (1). And from that day to the present hour the Romish Church in Ireland has been increasing its pretensions more and ever more. Having secured one advantage it quickly moves on to

(1) It is especially to be observed that, although Christianity has existed in Ireland for 1,431 years, the Church of Ireland has been free from the exercise of the Supremacy of the Pope for 1,052 years of that period. See 'Facts respecting the Present State of the Church in Ireland,' 5th Edition, p. 20.

secure another. It never rests satisfied with any advance already obtained; the cry is still give, give. In A.D. 1825 the Roman Catholic Archbishop (Murray) of Dublin, declared, before a Select Committee of the House of Commons, "that there was no *wish* on the part of the Roman Catholic "Clergy to disturb the present Establishment, or to partake "of any part of the wealth it enjoys;" and he added, "that "the Roman Catholic Clergy have not the least objection "to give the most full and entire assurance on that subject, "by any declaration that might be required of them." Bishop Doyle, the celebrated Roman Catholic Bishop of Leighlin, said on oath before the House of Lords, "I conceive that the removal of the disqualifications under which "Roman Catholics labour would lessen considerably those "feelings of opposition which they may at present entertain "with regard to the Establishment. The country would "settle down into a *habit of quiet*." (2) In A.D. 1826, the thirty Roman Catholic Bishops of Ireland declared on oath "that they disclaim, disavow, and solemnly abjure, any "intention to subvert the present Church Establishment "for the purpose of substituting a Catholic Establishment "in its stead. And further, they SWEAR that they will "not exercise any privilege to which they are or *may be* "*entitled*, to disturb and weaken the Protestant religion "and Protestant Government in Ireland." Such were the fair promises and solemn oaths by which a hesitating Parliament was induced to grant the full privileges of citizenship to their Roman Catholic fellow subjects. The Roman Catholic Bishops, on behalf of themselves and the whole Roman Catholic body in

---

(2) On this head it is worth referring to the recent reprint, Hayes, Lyall place, price 6d.—of "Roman Catholic Principles in reference to God and the King," under the title of "The Catholic Eirenicon."

Ireland, solemnly promised that they would not use any power they then had, or any to which they might become entitled to weaken or subvert the Established Church in that country. How have they kept that promise? How have they used the power they have since obtained? Scarcely was the ink of the Royal signature to the Emancipation Act dry than an agitation against the Irish Church, under the able leadership of Daniel O'Connell, was commenced, which only ended when ten Bishoprics of the Irish Church were suspended, and a fourth part of her remaining revenues confiscated. And who were the chief supporters—the ardent abettors of O'Connell in his crusade against the Church? The Roman Catholic Bishops and Clergy of Ireland. Who are now the founders of a so-called National Association "for DEMANDING the disendowment "of the Established Church in Ireland?" The same Roman Catholic Bishops and Clergy. They know well that the parochial system of the Irish Church is the one great impediment to their obtaining undivided sway over at least three-fourths of Ireland. They know well that it is the one great safeguard and protection of the scattered Churchmen of the South and West, who have now in every parish a centre of loyalty and Churchmanship round which they can rally in every hour of danger. They know, and daily feel this, and therefore they have resolved to make one bold and determined effort to rid themselves of it for ever. Should they succeed, whose would be the gain? Their's, and their's alone. England's hold on Ireland would be effectually weakened;—Rome's grasp of it effectually tightened. At present the Irish Church is the one chief means of maintaining that intercommunication between Englishmen and Irishmen on which the connexion between the two countries mainly depends. Irish Bishops sit in the House of Lords, and English graduates hold preferment in Ireland. We have lately seen one of the brightest ornaments of English literature transferred from an English Deanery to an Irish Archbishopric, whilst his predecessor in his See had been the Head of a Hall in Oxford.. The two Irish Primates and the present Bishop of Derry are all graduates of Trinity College, Cambridge. Disendow the Irish Church and this healthful interchange would cease at once. *Irish* graduates would doubtless cross the Channel in ever increasing numbers, but how many English graduates would cast in their lot with the poverty-stricken dis-established Church of Ireland ? Some no doubt there would be to whom the urgent need would of itself be call enough. But these could not be many. No :—if ever the people of England and Ireland are to be united in the bonds of cordial friendship, and a real national unity (to say nothing of a common faith), the Irish Church is undoubtedly the mediator through which that reconciliation must take place. That unity is not accomplished yet, but we are nearer to it than we were. On the other hand, displace the Established Church from the position she has held for nearly seven centuries (3), let Ireland, as regards the State, be left without any National religion, and a most effectual step will have been taken to make the wished-for reconciliation impossible. The Romish Church, the only real impediments to her supremacy removed, will then be able to dictate the terms on which the Government shall obtain peace in Ireland. The silent restraining power which the Church now exercises will never be fully appreciated till England suicidally removes it. The Irish people have never yet been taught to regard the Irish

---

(3) The Irish Church was first connected with the State by Henry II. in 1172 A.D.

Church as the old Catholic Church of Ireland. Rome has always told them that the true old Irish Church is the same with the Roman Communion in Ireland, and they have as yet believed her, and the language of English writers and statesmen has helped Rome to fasten this delusion on the people of Ireland. Once let Irishmen be convinced that the present Church of Rome in Ireland has no connexion with the old Church of S. Patrick, once let them realise that the only true successors of the old Catholic Bishops of Ireland are the Bishops of the Reformed Irish Church, and the power of Rome in Ireland will be shaken to its foundation, and a most effectual step will have been taken towards gathering the people of Ireland into the fold of the ancient Catholic Church of Ireland, from which so many of them are now separated.

VI.

THE SOCIAL ASPECT OF THE IRISH CHURCH QUESTION.

THERE is no public body in existence the defects of which are so well known as those of the Church in Ireland. For more than forty years she has been the constant object of Royal Commissioners' reports and Parliamentary inquiry. The religious population of every parish down to the minutest sub-division, the gross and net income of every single Bishop and Clergyman, the area of every benefice, has been fully and accurately ascertained, arranged, and classified. No weak point has been left in the shade, no short-comings have been concealed, all has been paraded before the world ; the worst that could be said of her has been said ; the worst that can be known of her is fully known.

Through such an ordeal as this what public body could pass unscathed ? And when it is remembered that those who have been nourished in her bosom and now eat of her bread have been amongst the foremost to bring to light her supposed defects, and have thus sounded all her imperfections trumpet-tongued through the land, can we wonder that a false impression has gone abroad respecting her, and that anomalies inherent in a National Church situated as she is, have been mistaken for abuses, and that evils arising from political mismanagement, in the origin of which she had no share, have been freely laid to her charge.

"Inequalities, no doubt, exist both in population and "in income, but such difficulties appear to be unavoidable, "and to exist, to some extent, in every Church Establish- "ment. That such anomalies should be remedied (so far "as they can be safely and wisely remedied) none are "more anxious than the Bishops of the Church. *It is,* "*however, much easier to point out a defect than to devise* "*such a remedy as would not presently entail greater evils* "*than it sought to remove.*"(1) We would commend these weighty words of the Primate of Ireland to the attentive consideration of those would-be Church Reformers, who, restless under the stinging imputations of the Church's enemies, are ever proposing delusive theories of reform, not one of which is capable of being carried out into practice, with the vain hope of averting a danger which arises from no desire for the Church's greater efficiency, but from the determinate purpose of procuring, if possible, her downfall as the Established Church of the country, first in Ireland and then in England.

In 1860, when the Government brought into Parliament a bill for regulating the then pending Census of 1861, it was proposed to ascertain the actual numbers of all the religious bodies in the United Kingdom. Such a proposition was vigorously and successfully opposed by the English Dissenters. They had their own reasons for objecting to be counted, and counted they were not. But the clause enjoining such an enumeration in Ireland was retained, and the result has been a census upon the basis of which the present attack on the Irish Church is nominally based, nominally we say, for the real force of

(1) Charge of Archbishop Armagh for 1864. Second Edition. P. 20.

the attack comes from the voluntary party in England, and not from the Roman Catholics of Ireland. It was originated by them under the auspices of Mr Dillwyn long before the formation of the so-called National Roman Catholic Association in Dublin.

The Roman Catholic Bishops and Priests, and the few leading demagogues who are joined with them in the ranks of the National Association, would be utterly powerless but for their English allies ; for the mass of the Roman Catholic population of Ireland cares nothing about the matter, and in nowise feels the Established Church to be a grievance, as the Fenian outbreak has clearly shown. Roman Catholic Priests, then, and English Protestant Dissenters have joined together for the purpose of obtaining, if possible, the destruction of the Established Church in Ireland that they may march over its ruins to a successful assault on the Established Church in England, and the one staple argument which they are ever presenting before the public in every possible shape and form is, that the Roman Catholics are the great majority of the people of Ireland, and that because they are so, they should be placed on a footing of equality with the Established Church in that country—in other words, that either the Roman Catholic Church should be endowed, or that the Irish Church should be despoiled of her property and disinherited.

Now, in considering this question, it is well to remember that in every country the number of the landed proprietors and educated classes, upon whom its prosperity and progress chiefly depends, must ever be few in number when compared with the masses of which the great majority of the population is composed. It is far from improbable that if the true numbers of those who are connected or sympathize with the Fenian conspiracy could be ascertained, they would be found far to outnumber the loyal and faithful subjects of the Queen in Ireland, but who in his senses would therefore argue that the Irish Republic should forthwith be established? Yet this is just the argument which we hear resounding on all sides for the destruction of the Irish Church as an Establishment. She is the Church, it is said, of a miserable minority, therefore down with her, down with her, even to the ground! Yet the Irish Church contains within her fold the very great majority of the nobility, gentry, landed proprietors, and members of learned professions in Ireland; 90 per cent. of the soil of Ireland is owned by Protestants. Of all the Irish Peers *nine* only are Roman Catholics, a tenth only of the landed proprietors belong to that Church, 28 per cent. only of the barristers of Ireland are Roman Catholics, whilst the greater majority of physicians and lawyers and all other learned professions are Protestant; and Dr Hume, in his accurate analysis of the Census of 1861, has clearly shown that whenever *skilled* labour is required Protestants are greatly in the ascendancy; and where mere manual labour suffices, there a large Roman Catholic majority is found. To take only one instance of many, the great majority of coach and car-*makers* are Protestants, whilst the great majority of coach and car-*drivers* are Roman Catholics.

We would gladly have been spared entering into these details had not the argument so constantly put forward of numbers being on the side of the Roman Catholics, rendered it necessary that we should do so. If mere numbers are to be the only standard by which an Establishment is to be judged, then it is evident that neither the Established Kirk in Scotland nor the Church in Wales can for a moment be defended as the Established religion of these countries; if the Irish Church falls before an argument such as this, the Scottish and Welsh Establishments must forthwith share its fate. The Irish Church is as much an integral part of the United Church as the Church in Wales; and if great principles are thus to be decided by mere numerical majorities, if we are to preserve any national religion at all, we must soon have to regulate it anew, according to the result of each successive Census!

Can we, then, for a moment suppose that a Church which comprehends the great majority of the leading classes of the community can be overthrown without a social revolution? Under the existing circumstances of Ireland, can it be prudent, or even safe, to excite in the minds of those who are the warmest and most loyal supporters of English rule, feelings of dissatisfaction and discontent? Can it be right to deprive at one stroke 700,000 Churchmen of all the means of grace, and leave them without any provision save that which they can themselves provide for their spiritual needs? Can it be consistent with *sound policy*, to say nothing of the principles of justice, to leave the scattered Churchmen of the South and West of Ireland, few in number it may be, but the very salt of the country as regards its allegiance to our Sovereign, without that pastoral care and those spiritual ministrations to which for centuries they have been accustomed? Are we prepared wholly to withdraw that silent restraining influence which the parochial Clergyman now exercises in every part of Ireland, and hand over three at least of the four Provinces to the uncontrolled dominion of the most Ultramontane and Papal Priesthood in Europe? Yet all this, and much more, will be accomplished by the downfall of the Established Church in Ireland. The blow would eventually fall with far heavier weight upon the Lay Churchmen of Ireland than upon the Clergy. The former have a far greater and more permanent interest in the temporalities of the Church than the latter. The Clergyman's pecuniary interest in his parish is necessarily of a temporary nature.

> "It soon becomes a story little known,
> That once he called the parsonage house his own."

But the landlord remains, and he and his children and his children's children will suffer if the Church's heritage is given over to the spoiler, and the House of God, from which for so long a period has ascended the hallowed words and pure faith of our Church's Liturgy, be left silent and desolate, a reproachful monument to his posterity of the faithlessness of that generation which had not the spirit to defend the inheritance that GOD had given them, or the self-denial to make any sacrifice for their MASTER's sake.

The time, therefore, has decidedly come when it imperatively behoves Churchmen on both sides the Channel thoroughly to consider the results that will follow from the disendowment of the Church in Ireland. Those who are leading on the attack seek as much as possible to divert public attention from this subject; yet it is of the greatest importance that it should be maturely considered by all. Ireland is at present in a transition state; between 1834 and 1861 the Roman Catholic population was diminished by two millions, and in the four years which have elapsed since the last census, more than 350,000 emigrants have left its shores. During the twenty-seven years above mentioned the Roman Catholics of Ireland lost nearly a *third* of their whole number, and should the emigration continue merely at its *present* rate—and it is probable that when the Fenian conspiracy is fully suppressed it will largely increase—the population of Ireland, by the next Census of 1871, will be again largely diminished. With a population in a state of such rapid transition, it is evident that no worse time could be chosen to propose a fundamental constitutional change than the present. In a few years, when public confidence is restored, and English capital finds its way back into Ireland, the religious aspects of whole districts may be changed, as has been the case already in a minor degree in some parts of the country ; nor can we think that it will tend to increase the prosperity of Ireland, or induce Englishmen to settle there, if the Irish branch of the United Church should be deprived of her revenues, and the burden of supporting her Churches and Clergy be placed entirely upon her own members. Nor should it be forgotten that the Churchmen of Ireland have ever been the stronghold of loyalty and obedience to the law in that kingdom. Whatever may happen to their Church revenues, loyal, no doubt, they would ever remain. But they will, in a great measure, be deprived of the means of encouraging loyalty amongst the people of remote districts of the land, where it is most necessary that it should be preserved. One of the first results that must undoubtedly follow from the dis-endowment of the Irish Church would be the withdrawal of the parochial Clergy from these poorer districts, whose inhabitants could not afford a maintenance for their pastor, and the sad results, morally, socially, and politically, that would ensue, it is not needful to dwell upon here. In many cases also the landlord, finding himself deprived of his intimate friend, and the spiritual instructor of his children, and the active ministrations of his own Church, would place his property in the hands of an agent, and swell the already large number of absentee proprietors. Nor can we imagine anything more detrimental to the social prosperity of a country situated such as Ireland is, than the passing of a measure which would deprive it of twelve resident noblemen and 1,500 resident gentry—for such are her Bishops and beneficed Clergy (to say nothing of the 662 Curates),—whose whole income, both private and professional, is spent in the country, and whose time and energies are entirely devoted to the spiritual and temporal welfare of its people. We trust that the statesmen and people of England will calmly and thoughtfully consider this aspect of the question; upon them the future of the Church in Ireland mainly rests. If they permit her endowments to be confiscated, centuries must elapse before the Church can regain that influence for good which she now possesses there; if they, on the other hand, refuse to give her over to the spoiler, and preserve intact the ancient heritage of the Church in Ireland, do not her renovated Cathedrals, her almost daily restored parish churches, and the energy, faithfulness, and devotion of her Clergy, give good promise that, by the blessing of the Great Head of the Church, a happy and prosperous future lies before her?

VII.

STATISTICS OF THE IRISH CHURCH.

As time goes on the real importance of the Irish Church question is beginning more and more to be realized. Statesmen are carefully considering it, and Churchmen on both sides of the Channel are anxious for accurate information respecting it. It is now seen that the future of the Reformed faith in Ireland greatly depends on the manner in which this question is settled ; and that if the Established Church by being disendowed is withdrawn from the remote districts of the country, no long time will elapse before three out of the four provinces of Ireland (with the exception of the large towns) will be entirely in the hands of Rome. It becomes, therefore, a matter of increasing importance that Churchmen in general should have the means of forming a fair and trustworthy opinion for themselves as to what the state of the Irish Church really is ; and this want, as far as regards the statistics of the question, we shall now endeavour in some measure to supply.

But we must premise in the first place that the true position which the Church holds in Ireland does not depend merely upon the number of her members. As regards population she is in an acknowledged minority when compared with the Roman Catholics of Ireland. But if ever there was a case in which a minority deserved to be weighed, as well as counted, it is this. The Church population of Ireland comprises nearly eight-ninths of the landed proprietors and the great majority of the learned professions, and therefore the Church contains the social and intellectual leaders of the nation, with few exceptions, within her pale; and if an Established Church is to be preserved in a country at all, that Church should be the Church of the governing classes, and not of the mere mass of the population, who naturally, in social and political matters, follow the lead of those placed over them.

With these preliminary observations let us proceed to consider the question now immediately before us.

The total population of Ireland during the last two centuries has been as follows:

1672	1,320,000
1767	2,544,276
1805	5,395,456
1834	7,954,100
1841	8,196,597
1851	6,574,278
1861	5,798,967

It will thus be seen that up to 1841 the population was steadily and rapidly increasing, but during the decade of 1841-1851, famine and pestilence, followed by emigration, diminished the population by no less than 1,622,319. The emigration continued with scarcely abated force during the next ten years, so that in 1861 Ireland contained 775,311 less inhabitants even than 1851. The whole loss between 1841 and 1861 was 2,397,630, or in round numbers 2,400,000. It is estimated that between April, 1861, and 31st of Dec., 1864, the total number of emigrants from

Ireland was 351,572, but as during that period there has been a large increase of births over deaths, the total population of Ireland on Dec. 31, 1864, was estimated at 5,673,424, or a loss of 125,543, since April, 1861.(1)

Now, these returns show that the population of Ireland is still rapidly diminishing, and that the country is, therefore, in a transition state, and we may expect that, when the Fenian bubble has finally burst, a large exodus of its deluded followers will take place, and the population of Ireland be still further reduced.

It is evident, therefore, that any legislation, respecting the Irish Church, which may take place during such a period of transition as that through which Ireland is now passing, may, unless great care is taken, result in permanent injury to the welfare of that country, especially when we remember that the relative position of Protestants and Roman Catholics in Ireland is undergoing a great, though little considered, change, as we shall now proceed to show.

In 1834 an enumeration of the people of Ireland according to their religious profession was taken. This was rather a compilation than a census. The regular census had been taken in 1831, and in 1834 the Commissioners appointed for the purpose "made the population returns of "1831 the basis of their operations, after having duly "considered the great expense, the prospect of delay, and "other inconveniences incidental to an entirely new "enumeration;" and they thus succeeded in compiling a census which, the Commissioners of 1861 are themselves obliged to confess, is "defective and inaccurate *in many "respects.*" (Report, p. 4.) And yet, be it observed, it is on the comparison of "this defective and inaccurate"

---

(1) For particulars see 'Thom's Official Directory' for 1866.—P. 703.

census of 1834 with that of 1861, and the result derived therefrom, that much of the present attack on the Irish Church is ostensibly based. We say "ostensibly based" because the real attack on the Established Church in Ireland arises, not from the smallness of the number of its members, but on that determined opposition to all union between Church and State, which is the chief characteristic of English political dissent, as well as on that energetic and vigorous effort which the Church of Rome is now making to become supreme in Ireland in all matters, educational as well as religious. The Established Church has ever been the greatest obstacle to this attempted supremacy of Rome, and therefore no effort will be spared to remove her from the position which she has held for so many centuries.

According to the compilation of 1834 the religious population of Ireland was as follows :

			Per cent.
Established Church	-	853,160	or 10·7.
Roman Catholics -	-	6,436,060	or 80·9.
Presbyterians -	-	643,058	or 8·1.
Protestant Dissenters	-	21,822	or 0·3.
		7,954,100	

Amongst the members of the Established Church, however, in 1834, the Wesleyan Methodists, "by a peculiarity "of their constitution" (Census Report of 1861, p. 5), were included. So that the real number of members of the Church in 1834 was 809,761, and not 853,160. It is important to bear this circumstance in mind, as most erroneous calculations have been made on the supposition that the Church population was diminished by 159,803 between 1834 and 1861 ; the truth is, the Church only lost

114,404, whilst the whole population of the country was diminished during that period by 2,155,133.

In 1861 the population of Ireland, arranged according to the various religious denominations, was returned as follows :—

Established Church	693,357	or 11·9 per cent.
Roman Catholics .	4,505,265	or 77·7 „
Presbyterians .	523,291	or 9·0 „
Protestant Dissenters	76,661	or 1·4 „
Jews	393	
	5,798,967	

It will thus be seen that whilst the Roman Catholic population of Ireland was diminished by a third, the Presbyterian by between a fifth and a sixth, the Church lost only between a seventh and an eighth, so that although all suffered a diminution of their actual numbers, the Church lost far less in proportion than the Roman Catholics, and considerably less than the Presbyterians. Moreover, it is worthy of especial observation that the proportion per cent. of the Church population has risen in twenty-one Dioceses out of the thirty-two in Ireland, whilst the Roman Catholic population has decreased in thirty Dioceses out of the thirty-two during the same period. So little truth is there in the assertion so pertinaciously put forward, and too commonly believed in, that the hold of the Church on the country is diminishing, whereas the truth is, that one of the most pressing causes of the present movement against her is the great increase of earnest Church work and sound and faithful teaching which is manifest of late years throughout the land.

The Census Commissioners of 1861 have shown how

little the deliberate statements of such reports may be depended on, when they declare that there has been an increase of 251·3 per cent of Protestant Dissenters in Ireland since 1834. A more fallacious statement could scarcely have been made. It has been clearly shown (2) that there has been a *decrease* of 22·4 per cent. of Protestant Dissenters instead of an increase, so that the Census Commissioners, in their anxiety to magnify the progress of Protestant Dissenters in Ireland during the last quarter of a century, made a miscalculation of not less than 273·4 per cent. Let this be a warning to all who are inclined without examination to depend on the supposed accuracy of Census returns!

As the revenues of the Irish Church have of late formed a fruitful subject of discussion, and from the different accounts published we should be disposed to think that great difficulties existed in the way of ascertaining their actual value, did we not know that the gross and net value of all the Bishoprics, and of every living over 300*l.* a year is annually returned to the Ecclesiastical Commissioners, and that as far at least as these are concerned there can be no difficulty whatever. But there are only 440 livings over 300*l.* a year, and there remains 1,070 under that number. The gross value of these latter livings are known, but their net value it is not possible to ascertain, as no return exists from which it can be obtained. It is satisfactory, however, to remember, that any calculations based on the returns already made to Parliament rather over-estimate than under-estimate the income of the Irish Clergy, and it is well to bear this in mind, as there is scarcely any part of the Irish Church question which has

---

(2) See Archbishop of Armagh's Charge of 1864, pp. 17 and 48; and 'Facts respecting the Irish Church,' 5th Edition, p. 8.

been so persistently and constantly misrepresented as this.

A great difference frequently exists between the nominal and real value of an Irish benefice. The cause of this is easily ascertained, and the diminution of income which ensues in consequence of the taxes payable by the Clergy is often of a very serious nature. It is often forgotten, in considering this subject, that the charges paid by the Church rate in England, in Ireland come out of the pockets of the Clergy. All livings over 300*l.* a year pay a tax varying from 5 to 15 per cent. according to annual value, and the Bishoprics are taxed in like manner. In 1864 this tax (including the charges on the Sees of Armagh and Derry) realized no less than 27,188*l.*, no inconsiderable sum to be raised annually by a single tax on twelve Bishoprics and 440 benefices. But this is only a single item of a long account. The Clergy pay the full poor rate on the gross rent charge, no deductions being allowed, whilst other landlords pay but half, and the tenants the other half. During the famine year, the poor rate was known to exceed in some districts the whole of the Incumbent's stipend, and it usually averages 10 per cent. of his income. In addition to this a tax is paid to the Diocesan School, and the new Ecclesiastical Courts and Registration Act requires all Incumbents to pay a penny in the pound in lieu of visitation fees. When these taxes are added together they will be found in the aggregate to amount to no inconsiderable sum.

It has of late been asserted that the value of glebe houses should be included amongst the revenues of the Irish Church. However plausible this may appear at first sight, nothing could be more unfair than such a calculation. The glebe houses in Ireland have been erected either at the expense of the present Incumbents or of their predecessors. When a Clergyman is inducted into a living with a glebe house, he usually has *to pay out of his own pocket* a large portion of the original cost of building the house, in the shape of a building charge payable to his predecessor or his representatives, in addition to which an annual instalment in many cases has to be paid to the Ecclesiastical Commissioners in liquidation of money borrowed for the building of the house. The incumbent is also under the heavy liability of having to keep the glebe house in thorough repair and free from ecclesiastical dilapidation, and may therefore be considered rather to have purchased the use of the house during his incumbency, than to possess it in right of his benefice. To include, therefore, the annual value of the house in his yearly income would be unjust, as well as fallacious.

The Ecclesiastical Commissioners, the general accuracy of whose returns may thoroughly be relied on, estimate "the gross revenue of the Established Church in Ireland "(including bishoprics and dignities and livings, whether "derived from lands, rent charges, or any other source) at "586,428*l.* 8s. 1d. per annum. The net value, after "deductions *directed by law* in estimating the Ecclesias-"tical tax payable to the Commissioners, is 448,943*l.* 15s. "10d." But, the Commissioners add, "there are further "deductions *to a considerable amount* upon livings under "300*l.* a year, which are about 1,070 out of a total of "1,510, the particulars of which deductions are officially "unknown to the Ecclesiastical Commissioners, such livings "not being liable to tax." It is evident, then, that the sum returned by the Commissioners as the net income of the Irish Bishops and Clergy is considerably in excess of its real amount.

Of the above annual revenue the Bishops receive 55,110*l.*, he beneficed Clergy 393,833*l.* The incumbents being

1,510, this would give an average of 260*l*. a year to each, or allowing 15*l*. for the deductions from the 1,070 livings mentioned above (which would be a small average) their actual income does not exceed 245*l*. a year each.

It will thus be seen that no real difficulty exists in ascertaining what are the actual incomes of the Irish Bishops and Clergy.

But it has been argued that in order to ascertain what the real revenues of the Irish Church are, the annual incomes of the Ecclesiastical Commissioners should be added to those of the Bishops and Clergy. It therefore becomes necessary to examine how that income is obtained.

The income of the Ecclesiastical Commissioners for 1864 arose from the following sources:

	£
Suppressed See Estates - - -	58,127
Suspended Benefices and dignities - -	19,162
Tax on Bishoprics and Benefices, and annual charge on Sees of Armagh and Derry -	27,187
Interest on Government Securities, &c. -	7,460
	£111,936

Of this sum the Ecclesiastical Commissioners pay 12,500*l*. a year to the Clergy in lieu of Ministers' money, and also some 8,000*l*. a year in augmentation of small livings, and for disappropriated tithes; both of which sums have been included in the annual incomes of the respective Incumbents. The total of these items, viz., 20,500*l*., must therefore be deducted before the balance which is to be added to the Church's revenue on account of the income of the Ecclesiastical Commissioners can be ascertained. This would leave 91,436*l*. a year, which, if added to the net incomes of the Bishops and Clergy, viz., 448,943*l*. (the deductions from the 1,070 livings under 300*l*. not being made), would give 540,379*l*. as the annual available income of the Irish Church, including that of the Ecclesiastical Commissioners (3).

As regards the augmentation of the Clergyman's income by means of pew rents, such payments, with the exception of a few proprietary Chapels in some of the larger towns, we are thankful to record, are totally unknown in Ireland. *All the seats in the parish Churches of Ireland are free.* The aggregate income, therefore, derived by the Irish Clergy from pew rents must be very inconsiderable, and in every case they depend so much upon the popularity of the individual Clergyman, that it would be impossible to reckon upon them as a permanent source of income.

No Church or vestry rates are now paid in Ireland. The requisites for Divine service, the salaries of the clerks and sextons, the fuel for warming, the means for lighting the Churches, and the Elements for the Holy Communion, are all paid out of Church funds provided by the suppression of ten Bishoprics and various benefices, and by an annual tax on the existing Bishops and Clergy. The Church Temporalities Act thus relieved the Laity from all payments for Church purposes, whilst it placed a new and unwonted burden on the Clergy. It was estimated by Lord Althorp in 1834 that the vestry cess alone produced 90,000*l*. a year, and this, as soon as the Church Temporalities Act came into operation, passed into the pockets of the Laity, together with 25 per cent. of the rent charge of all Ireland. The Clergy of the Irish Church have thus lost

(3) I am indebted to Archdeacon Hincks for having pointed out an oversight in the above calculation, as it originally appeared, but which is now corrected in the text.

within the last thirty years at least 250,000*l.* of annual income. We should have thought that would have satisfied the most ardent Irish Church Reformer, but it is now evident that nothing but the total abolition of the Established Church is aimed at by those who are conducting the present attack on her temporalities.

But whilst the income of the Irish Church has thus been continually decreased, she has earnestly and not unsuccessfully laboured with diminished means to maintain efficiency in every department of her work. It will be seen from the following authentic returns that she has not laboured in vain :

	Clergy.	Churches.	Benefices.	Glebe Houses.
1806 (4)	1,253	1,029	1,181	295
1826 (5)	1,977	1,192	1,396	768
1864 (6)	2,172	1,579	1,510	978

Since 1806, then, the Irish Clergy have increased by 919, the Churches by 550, the Benefices (chiefly through the dissolving of unions) by 329, and the Glebe Houses by 683, it cannot, therefore, be maintained that the Irish Church is not fully alive to the responsibilities which rest upon her.

We earnestly trust that Churchmen who desire that the Reformed Faith of our primitive and Apostolic Church should at least not recede from the ground it now holds in Ireland, will make themselves fully acquainted with the real state and position of the Church in that country. No

(4) 'Report of Commission of Ecclesiastical Inquiry,' 1807.

(5) J. C. Erck's 'Ecclesiastical Register.'

(6) 'Parliamentary Return,' 1864.

See also 'Facts respecting the present State of the Church in Ireland.' Fifth Edition. Page 18.

efforts have been, or will be wanting to excite popular prejudices against her. Misrepresentations respecting her which have been again and again exposed, are again and again unblushingly repeated, and therefore it behoves all who desire to form a correct opinion of this important subject to examine the facts of the case for themselves, and to be satisfied with nothing less than a personal examination of the present state and position of the Church in Ireland.

VIII.

THE TRUE PRINCIPLES ON WHICH THE IRISH CHURCH IS TO BE MAINTAINED.

The time is not far distant when all Churchmen who earnestly desire the prosperity and advancement of the National Church of these kingdoms will find themselves compelled seriously to consider what their duty is with regard to that branch of the United Church which is now established in Ireland. Political Dissenters in England and the Roman Catholic Bishops and Clergy of Ireland are banded together to procure her downfall. Shall we be doing our duty to Christ and His Church, if we permit their undeniably earnest and vigorous exertions to succeed without one united effort on our part to avert the threatened danger? Shall we allow the only religious body in Ireland, which teaches alike Apostolic truth, and maintains Apostolic order, which is one in doctrine, government, and discipline, with our own Church, to be deprived of the means of teaching those doctrines, and upholding that discipline in the remote districts of the land, whilst we stand by and make no sign? Can we even, without danger to ourselves, allow a sister Church, united to the State by the same bonds of union as we are, to be shorn of her temporalities, on the sole plea that she is not the Church of the majority of the nation? Will not principles thus be established which in no long period the opponents of all State connexion in England will not be slow to apply to ourselves? And even if we had no personal interest in the matter as regards our own Church, can it be right, can it be just, is it consonant with the principles which we all hold so dear, or with our national character, of which we are so greatly proud, to leave the Church in Ireland, the old Catholic Church of that country, to be despoiled by her enemies, whilst we have it in our power to aid, to succour, and successfully defend her?

Such are the questions which we are persuaded the course of events will soon bring home to the minds of all earnest Churchmen. The Irish Church question cannot remain long in the position it now occupies; neither is it desirable even for the Church's sake that it should so do. It must be determined in one way or another, and the settlement when it comes should, as far as possible, be final. It is most injurious to the best interests of the community, that such a fundamental question should be left in a state of uncertainty. It keeps agitation alive, whilst it distracts the attention and weakens the energies of the Clergy.

It may be well then briefly to consider the principles on which the Irish Church should be maintained, and the probable consequences that would follow, should she no longer remain the Established Church of Ireland.

I. The chief reason undoubtedly why the Irish Church should be maintained in her present position in Ireland is, that "she is the pillar and ground of the truth" in that country. Pre-eminently the Church of Ireland is a city set on a hill, a light which cannot be hid. Whilst inculcating on her own members the sound Scriptural and primitive teaching of the Prayer Book, she presents, on the one hand, to the Irish Romanist a Church, pure in her doctrine, and Catholic in her faith; and on the other, to the Irish Dissenter she offers a form of sound words in her Liturgy, unrivalled in the world, and the Apostolic ministry. If ever the true faith of CHRIST, free from Romish and Puritan error, is to become the belief of the great mass of the Irish people (and are we yet prepared altogether to resign the hope that one day this may be the case?) it must be through the instrumentality of the Church that this great healing must be effected. The Church has never yet been placed in her true position before the eyes of the great mass of the Irish people. They have been taught to look upon her as an alien Church—the Church of their conquerors—as the English Church in Ireland, rather than as she is, the true old Catholic Church of the country. Gradually yet surely this delusion is passing away. The Irish Clergy are more and more plainly bringing before their people the true position their Church holds, and the more they appreciate this truth, the more they will learn to love and respect her. At present the Roman Catholics scornfully laugh at the teaching of this great truth ; but the time is not far distant when they will find that ridicule is no match for truth, and that if the Church of Rome is to retain her hold on the affections of the Irish people, she must *prove* (if she can) as well as assert, that she is the old Church of the country.

II. But the Irish Church is to be maintained in her present position, not merely for the sake of promoting the spiritual and moral welfare of her own members, not merely because in Ireland she is the depository of Primitive and Catholic truth, but also because it is solely through her instrumentality that Christian union can ever be brought about in Ireland. If Churchman, and Romanist, and Presbyterian are ever to be united in one communion, it is only on the basis of the Church that such a union can be effected. Very rarely do we hear of Romanists becoming Presbyterians, or Presbyterians becoming Romanists, but we hear continually of Romanists and Presbyterians becoming Churchmen. The conversions on either side may be comparatively few in comparison with the members of either communion ; but the point to be considered is the direction in which these conversions take place, and we are fully persuaded, from our own experience, that if the principles of the Church were plainly, faithfully, wisely, and moderately set before the Irish Romanist, and the Irish Dissenter, the Church ere long would gain from both many members to her fold. Hitherto it must be acknowledged the Irish Church has been too polemical in her teaching, and this is doubtless one of the chief causes why she has not made a more favourable impression on those who are separated from her. A Church progresses more by a diligent and faithful inculcation of her own principles on her own members, than by any amount of vigorous attacks on her opponents, whilst her own members grow up ignorant of her teaching. In their zeal to make Roman Catholics, Protestants, it may be true that the Irish Clergy have too much neglected to make their own people sound and understanding Churchmen. But this evil is now clearly seen, and is in process of being remedied, and if the Synods of the Irish Church were once more quickened into life, and the Irish Bishops and Clergy were permitted to devise means for Church revival and Church extension, the day is not far distant, when the Irish Church would give proof of a life and vigour within her, such as would effectually answer those objectors, who complain of her want of expansive power, or of her ability to gain the affections of those who now are opposed to her.

III. Again, the Irish Church is to be maintained as the National Church in Ireland, because the honour of England is pledged to her being so. The Union of 1800 consisted of three parts,—it united two Kingdoms, two Parliaments, two Churches, into one United Kingdom, one United

Parliament, and one United Church. But the fundamental article of the treaty was the union of the two Churches. The Churchmen of Ireland were assured by the Government that if the Irish Church was completely incorporated with the Church of England "it would be placed on such "a strong and sure foundation as to be above every appre- "hension and fear from adverse interest, and from all the "fretting and irritating circumstances of its colonial "situation;" and it was not till it had been made "an "essential and fundamental part of the union," (1) that the united Church should be continued and preserved as "*the Established Church of England and Ireland*," that the Irish Bishops, as the representatives of the Church, agreed in Parliament to the Irish Church giving up its separate and independent existence, and become one with the Church in England.

Can we for a moment believe that either the Lords Spiritual and Temporal, or the members of the Commons House in Parliament assembled in Dublin College Green, would ever for a moment have agreed to such a union if they could have foreseen that very little more than half a century afterwards it would be maintained in the united Parliament that, after all, this compact as regards the Church was but of a temporary nature, and was not by any means a fundamental and essential part "of the union?" If the union of the Churches can so easily be dissolved, why not also the union of the kingdoms? If the claims of Irish Protestants on the justice and equity of the British Parliament are to be treated with indifference and scorn, can we wonder if a future generation of Irish Protestants should come to think that such a Parliament has little claim on their confidence or support? If Parliament

---

(1) Speech of Lord Castlereagh on the union.

recklessly disturbs a national compact which solemnized the union of two nations, will it be a matter of surprise to any if the Church in the end is not the party which will principally suffer? Never, we verily believe, will Irishmen become in any way again united to demand a separate national existence till the full consequences of the disestablishment of the Irish Church are felt by Irish Protestants, and who then can say what will follow? The Irish Romanist and the English Voluntary may each for their own separate and distinct purpose now join together to demand the disendowment of the Irish Church; but it is for English statesmen to consider—each one calmly and thoughtfully for himself—what the final consequences of such a fatal step may be, when a Liberal Secretary of State has declared in his place in the House of Commons of such a scheme, "that the Irish Church is interwoven "with the constitution of the country, and could not be "subverted without a revolution," (2) which the Chancellor of the Exchequer declares "to be a nest of political "problems of the very greatest difficulty," and of which a Roman Catholic Judge, Mr Justice Shee, has written, "the Church by law established in Ireland is the Church "of a community everywhere considerable in respect of "property, rank, and intelligence; it is strong in a prescrip-"tion of three centuries, and in the support which it "derives from the supposed identity of its interests with "those of the Church of England. *Nothing short of a "convulsion, tearing up* BOTH *Establishments by the roots, "could accomplish its overthrow.*" (3)

IV. Another, and very cogent reason why the Established

---

(2) Sir George Grey's Speech, Jan. 29, 1863.

(3) 'The Irish Church: its History and Statistics.' Second Edition. Pp. 3, 24.

Church should be maintained in her present position is, that her disendowment would produce an amount of discontent amongst Protestants, and subsequent damage to the peace and advancement of the country which is now little thought of. The landlords of Ireland, with few exceptions, are Protestants. The Church is now their bond of union. Disestablish the Church. Throw the burden of maintaining her on the landlords, for on them in such a case it must, in most districts, principally fall, compel them as well to pay the full rent-charge to some secular purpose, and the result it is not difficult to foresee. At present the landlords have inherited or purchased their estates subject to the tithe rent-charge, and they receive 25 per cent. of it for becoming responsible for it to the Clergy, and therefore they pay it without a murmur. But let an Act of Parliament devote the whole of the rent-charge to some secular purpose (and Mr Gladstone is very careful to remind the Irish landlords that in such a case they must not hope to retain the 25 per cent. they now receive), let not only the burden of maintaining the Clergy of the Church who are to remain, but also that of repairing and building Churches, and of furnishing the requisites for Divine service now provided from Church funds be placed, as in such a case it must be, solely upon the laity ; and no sooner will they feel the unwonted burden than they will turn on those who have inflicted it, and, however vainly, it may now be hoped that Roman Catholic discontent in Ireland will be put a stop to by the disestablishment of the Church, it is plain and evident to all those who have carefully considered the matter that a Protestant discontent of no light or trifling kind will then be added to the other difficulties which future Governments will have to contend with in Ireland. Let, then, statesmen pause and consider well the consequences that will follow before they rashly introduce a new and fruitful element of discord into that unhappy country.

Be it remembered also that one of the chief difficulties of Ireland arises, not from a difference of religion, but of race, amongst its people. It is possible to turn a Roman Catholic into a Churchman, it is impossible to turn a Celt into a Saxon. You may give a sop to Cerberus in hopes of quieting him for a time, but the native dislike of England will ere long break out again with two-fold energy, and no sooner will the Irish Church have been sacrificed to popular clamour, than it will be found that, after all, the Irish land question was at the bottom of Irish discontent, and that their triumph over the Church has not satisfied her opponents, but only emboldened them to make further and more imperious demands.

V. Lastly, let it be borne in mind that the disendowment of the Irish Church means nothing less than the deliberate giving up of all hopes of permanently advancing the principles of the Reformation in Ireland. It is nothing less than voluntary resigning the religious teaching of the people of three out of the four provinces of Ireland, with the exception of the large towns, without any counteracting influence, into the hands of the most Ultramontane Priesthood in Europe. Disendow the Established Church, and in less than a quarter of a century the Reformed Church will be withdrawn from posts of vantage she now occupies, which it will require three centuries of earnest and persevering work to win back again from the hands of Rome. The Irish Roman Catholic Prelates, wise in their generation, see and know this, and therefore gladly make use of all the Protestants they can influence, to further their darling design of uncontrolled supremacy in Ireland, in all things educational and religious. The wonder is that any Protestants, especially dissenting Protestants, can be so blinded by their hatred of connexion of religion with the State, as to fight side by side with those whose object is, to give an effectual and, if possible, a deadly blow to the Reformed faith in Ireland, by the help of those whose chief boast is, that they faithfully maintain Protestant principles against "the "deadly errors" of Rome.

For all these reasons, then, because the Church is in Ireland the sole upholder of the Sacred and Scriptural teaching of our Reformed Church; because she is the only means by which any future union between Christians in Ireland, now unhappily divided, can be brought about; because her disendowment would be a violation of a solemn national compact, and therefore a stain on England's honour, and would not remove Roman Catholic dissatisfaction, whilst it would certainly produce a large amount of Protestant discontent which does not now exist; because her disestablishment would undo the work of centuries, and hand Ireland over politically and religiously into the hands of Rome; because the withdrawal of the endowments of the Irish Church would be but an encouragement to a more vigorous and united onslaught on those of the Church in England; above all, because it would deprive a large number of our fellow Churchmen, without any fault of their own, of the means of grace, and leave them in the utmost danger of becoming a prey to infidelity or Rome;—for these and many other reasons which are too numerous to mention here, we desire to see the Irish Church strengthened and maintained in the position she now holds, and which for seven centuries she has been in possession of.

It is sometimes brought as a charge against the defenders of the Irish Church, that they are opposed to all sincere attempts to remove the anomalies which exist in her, and from which no Established Church can be wholly free. This is, however, far from the true state of the case. Such persons are opposed to spoliation, but would gladly aid every well-considered and judicious scheme of Reform, when brought forward by competent authority, and which would increase the efficiency and augment for good the working of the Irish Church. But the object of the present attack is not reform, but abolition. This is openly and plainly avowed. The Roman Catholic Bishops (4) "demand the disendowment of the Established Church." Sir John Gray and those who act with him (5) "are fully "determined never to let this question rest until Church "ascendancy is abolished, and until perfect religious equa-"lity is established in Ireland."

We cannot therefore complain of reticence of speech in those who are attacking the Church, or of ignorance of the real objects they have in view. *Delenda est Carthago* is their motto; nothing less will satisfy them. If, then, Churchmen in general wish to see maintained in Ireland the true principles which our Church teaches, if they are unwilling that the Reformed faith in that country should recede from the position that it has held for centuries, they must be up and doing, they must be no longer lukewarm or indifferent with regard to her, they must be earnest and sincere, faithful and energetic in her cause, they must make some self-sacrifice, and exercise some self-denial for the sake of defending and upholding the Irish branch of CHRIST's Holy Catholic Church.

---

(4) Resolution of Dublin meeting, December, 1864.

(5) Speech in House of Commons, April 11, 1866.

INDEX.

www.ingramcontent.com/pod-product-compliance
Lightning Source LLC
Chambersburg PA
CBHW020255090426
42735CB00009B/1094

9783337125912